The GEM Principle

The GEM Principle

Six Steps to Creating a
High Performance Organization

Daniel Quinn Mills
Harvard University
Graduate School of Business Administration

omneo
An imprint of
Oliver Wight Publications, Inc.
85 Allen Martin Drive
Essex Junction, VT 05452

Table of Contents

Preface

New approaches to management and leadership have quickly taken hold in our dynamic business world. In recent years, most companies have restructured or reorganized, selecting their management programs from a range of diverse innovative alternatives. Many have adopted total quality management (TQM) initiatives; some have pursued continuous improvement; others have downsized or rightsized; still others have delayered or have introduced cross-functional teams; and numerous firms have ventured into the area of business process engineering—the effort to achieve a dramatic increase in productivity by radically reorganizing a part or process of a business. There is, however, one fundamental element underlying this diversity: the commitment to establish a greater degree of teamwork among employees, with more responsibility delegated across the organization; that is, the concept of *empowerment,* which acts as the atom from which the molecules of these different approaches are constructed. *The GEM Principle* examines this core concept, presenting six steps for high-performance organization as it narrates a fictional but realistic account of the problems faced by management in a typical American company.

Many business executives, most of them in companies very much like the one depicted in this book, are betting the futures of their organizations on the concept of empowerment. They find the idea so appealing because in a bitterly competitive marketplace, it offers hope for success. Empowerment also has attracted many politicians, providing them with a conceptual foundation on which to base their hopes for effective grassroots action in our society; in a world of distant and unresponsive government institutions, it promises to lend some power to the average individual. In fact, the word *empowerment* is now so widely used that it is rapidly becoming a buzzword, part of a cliché about more freedom for rank-and-file people in both the political world and the business world. Its popularity speaks of the great needs of our time. Although that popularity has also promoted a great deal of distrust, the bottom line is that those in power believe that empowerment will work. When a reporter asked Jack Welch, chairman of General Electric, why, if empowerment is so vital, "so many consider this stuff Mickey Mouse," he replied: "There is cynicism about this stuff in our society. But I think the people who run a lot of today's corporations believe in it. What are we doing this for? To be competitive. To win." ("He Brought GE to Life," *Newsweek,* November 30, 1992, p. 63).

Despite the popular use of the word *empowerment,* the concept is poorly understood by many people. Empowerment is much more than simply setting up teams in a company or establishing local councils in a district and then letting them make decisions and act independently. Instead, for empowerment to produce successful results, several conditions must be met, which themselves demand considerable effort to achieve. The reason for this is straightforward: In a complex organization, islands of empowerment must be coordinated and aligned with one another or the resulting conflict of direction and purpose will create chaos. Making sense of the whole through cooperation among the parts is the function of both political leadership and corporate management. Consequently, empowerment does not mean an end of the hierarchy of power, but rather a reduction in its size and a revision of its functions. For those of us who work in organizations that are experiencing change, understanding what the new empowered environment requires of us is critical to both the success of our careers and the success of our companies.

It is also vital that the cynicism about empowerment be understood for what it is: a basic misconception. Despite the egalitarian principles in which empowerment is so obviously rooted, some people who believe in workplace democracy nevertheless distrust it. Although it conveys the clear message that people should be free to act on their own, it has been denounced for its alleged implication that the many must be given power— "empowered"—by the few who possess it. But those who object on this basis confuse their aspirations with reality. In fact, in a world of large hierarchically organized institutions, power does tend to be concentrated in the hands of the few; however, if they do not relinquish some control, then there cannot be greater initiative for the many. The term *empowerment,* with its implication of delegation downward, is therefore in accord with reality.

Among the conditions most necessary for empowerment is a restructuring of the traditional hierarchy found in most large organizations. In the traditional setting, supervisors are charged with directing the work of subordinates in a way incompatible with empowerment. I have addressed the complex issue of restructuring in a previous book entitled *The Rebirth of the Corporation.* This current book, *The GEM Principle,* supplements *Rebirth* without repeating it. Together, the two volumes present a comprehensive view of how empowerment works in an organization, describing in depth the new structure of business—clusters or empowered teams (*Rebirth*)—and the new style of management that complements it—GEM management (*Empowerment*).

It is hoped that this book will contribute to the improvement of our organizations by helping readers understand better what empowerment entails and what conditions are necessary for its achievement. Although this concept is discussed in the context of business management, it should be remembered that the principles delineated here apply fully to government and offer hope not only for our business organizations but for our society as well.

The GEM Principle

Chapter 1

Doing More With Less:
The Management Challenge
of the Nineties

John Cardenas, an executive in a large corporation, was prepared to do some explaining when he called two department
managers, Susan Johnson and Charles LaRucca, into his office
for a meeting.

"We're going to be downsizing again," he told them.

"Oh, no!" Susan exclaimed. "Not again."

"Yes, again," Cardenas confirmed.

"And we're not going to get any reduction in our business
goals, are we?" Charles asked.

"No."

"That's the management problem of the Nineties, isn't it?"
Susan added. "You have to do as much or more with less—a
smaller budget, fewer people . . ."

"You're right," John agreed with a sympathetic smile. "But
you understand why, don't you?"

He got up from his chair and went to the white board on the
other side of his desk.

"First," he began to explain, "the business world is much
different than it was a few years ago. I went to an executive
seminar at a major university last month, and the participants
talked continually about two things: first, how much more rapidly
change occurs now than it did in the past, whether it be in
technology, economics, or national and global politicals; and
second, how very much more competitive every business is—and
nowhere more so than in the North American marketplace.

1

As he talked he wrote on the board:

- *Increased Competition*

- *More Rapid Change*

"To meet the competition and keep up with the increasing pace of change, we must do three things in our business: cut our costs, improve the quality of our products and services, and respond more quickly to our customers."

He wrote on the board:

- *Reduced Cost*
- *Increased Quality*

- *Enhanced Responsiveness*

He paused a moment to let Susan and Charles absorb what he had said; then he asked, "Now, how do we accomplish these things?"

Susan and Charles were silent.

"Well, we do several things," he said. "First, we downsize and delayer our organization to cut costs; then we set up programs like total quality management or market-driven quality to let everyone see that we're serious about improving the quality of our services and products; finally, we establish cross-functional teams of employees to break them out of the stove-pipe mentality of functioning as separate departments and to get them working together, and faster, so that we can be more responsive."

He wrote on the board:

- *Downsizing*
- *Delayering*
- *Total Quality Management*
- *Market-Driven Quality*
- *Increased Delegation*
- *Cross-Functional Teams*

"So that brings us to where we are today," Cardenas told his two subordinates.

2

"But where is all this taking us?" Charles blurted out. "We can't just keep downsizing and delayering forever and still keep doing more and more work at better quality levels."

Cardenas frowned at him. "To be frank," he said, "I don't know where all this will take us in the long term, but for now, it's what we're going to do. So let's talk about how to make this next round of cuts."

For two hours the three struggled to develop a plan for the upcoming cutbacks. Again and again they debated ways to save this person or that activity.

"It's as if all we're doing is trying to limit our losses," observed Susan with exasperation. "It's all damage control. We don't seem to be trying to achieve much anymore."

While listening to her comments, Charles was suddenly seized by the recollection of a seminar he'd attended a few years ago. "You know," he told the others, "I've a story that may give us a different perspective on this problem."

"Then by all means tell us," Cardenas said.

So Charles did.

CHARLES' STORY

Several years ago I attended a meeting with the management team of the division I was working in. Thirty or so of us gathered in a rather plain room, its walls lined with chairs and its floor covered with a dusty carpet. A facilitator had been brought in to conduct the session, and he began with an exercise.

He told us to think about the people who were present in the room. "Whom do you personally most admire?" he asked. "If I told you that over the next few days each of you had to work on an assignment with someone here, whom would you pick for a partner?" Then he had us write the name of the person on a slip of paper and pocket it.

"Now," he said, "I'd like each of you to go over to the person whose name is on that slip of paper in your pocket,

and when you've paired up with him or her, sit down together on the floor."

There was a lot of milling about and confusion as people sought out their partners and paired up, but soon everyone was seated.

The facilitator seemed pleased and began to walk among the pairs. He stopped and asked one executive, "Who are you with?"

"Joe," the executive answered.

Then the facilitator asked her whose name she had written on the slip of paper in her pocket. When the executive said "Joe," the facilitator nodded and moved on.

But before long he came upon a different situation.

"Who are you with?" he asked another executive, a man in his fifties.

The man said, "Cynthia."

This time when the facilitator asked whose name was on the slip of paper, he received an embarrassed reply.

"Anne," the executive replied with a tremor in his voice.

"So you're not with the person whose name you wrote down?" the facilitator asked.

When the man responded no, the facilitator asked him, "Why not?"

"Well," the man said, "Cynthia's a fine partner too."

It was clear that the man just wanted the facilitator to let the matter drop, but the facilitator wouldn't.

"I'm sure she is," he said, "but did you go over to Anne to see if she'd pair up with you?"

The man said yes, but when the facilitator asked if Anne had refused to be his partner, he found out that the man hadn't even asked her.

"Why not?" the facilitator asked.

The man said, "Well . . . there were a lot of other people around her."

The facilitator asked if she had been a popular choice.

"Yes," the man replied.

Then the facilitator went back to the question of why the executive hadn't asked Anne to be his partner.

"I just didn't," the man said. "There were other people there."

The facilitator seemed to get a little upset. He asked in a demanding tone of voice, "Did they stop you? Did someone push you away?"

The man replied, "No, not at all."

"Then why didn't you ask Anne to pair up with you?" the facilitator asked again. He was relentless.

The man, by now clearly exasperated, finally broke down and admitted, "I was afraid she would want to pair up with someone else, and I didn't want to get rejected."

The facilitator nodded his head appreciatively and thanked the executive. "I know that's an honest answer," he said.

Then he looked at the rest of us. We were all sitting on the floor, listening intently.

"This is only a game," he told us. His attention turned once again to the executive. "But how did you play the game? Did you play to win—to pair up with the person whose name you'd written down on that slip of paper? Or did you play it not to lose—to keep from being rejected or from having to accept failure?"

The executive looked somewhat shame-faced. "I guess I played it not to lose," he said. "I didn't play to win. I didn't take the chance."

Once again the facilitator addressed the entire group.

"How easy it is for each of us to play the game of enterprise not to win, but to protect what we already have. In this business, when we enter the competitive arena we already have jobs and departments. We want to make sure we don't lose anything, so we don't really play the game of enterprise to come out on top. We hedge our bets; we don't cooperate fully with others; we don't take risks that are necessary to be successful. In short, we don't play to win; instead, we play the game not to lose.

"And that, of course," he concluded, *"is not the way to win. You have to play to win."*

"The danger," Charles concluded, "is that in all this downsizing, if we don't figure out something new, we're going to spend all our time and effort trying not to lose—instead of playing to win."

John Cardenas' eyes lit up. "I couldn't agree with you more," he said. "I heard Indiana's great basketball coach, Bobby Knight, talking about this the other night. He was discussing winning and the desire to win, and he said, 'The desire to win is much less important than the desire to *prepare* to win!'

"When contestants go onto a sports field," John continued, "often they both have the desire to win. But the victory goes to those who have had the will to prepare to win—who are best conditioned, best trained, best drilled, best equipped. This is what Bobby Knight was talking about."

He turned back to Charles. "Your facilitator was right: We have to play to win, not focus our attention on trying not to lose. And Bobby Knight is right: We have to have the will not just to win, but more important, to *prepare* to win."

They discussed the matter for several more minutes; then Cardenas told them he had to attend another meeting but wanted to share something with them before he left.

"Do you remember the big new account that was on everyone's mind about a year and a half ago?" he asked.

Susan and Charles nodded.

"Well, the meeting is with the cross-functional team we put together to try to sell that account," he explained. "They worked on the project for over a year—spent more than a million dollars. They had tough competition too, from three other firms. To deal with that, we told them they were empowered to do whatever they thought was necessary to win, within our principles, of course. And have they been independent! They've adopted two rules: first, to ensure that no one pulls rank in a team meeting, they require you to check your badge before the meeting starts— every-one is an equal participant; second, unless you've been in contact with the customer, you're not allowed to make any decisions—outside executives can't suddenly step in and take over."

The two managers looked incredulously at their boss.

"Have they really held to that?" Susan asked in amazement.

"Yes, they have," Cardenas said with a smile, his eyebrows raised as if he were as surprised as she. "I'll give you an example.

"At one point our three competitors brought in their chief executive officers to meet with the customer's chief executive officer. It was obvious they were trying to get an advantage over one another—and us.

"Our team met to decide what to do. They asked our CEO if he would come to a meeting with the CEO of the customer, and he responded favorably. Then they asked the customer's procurement group if it would be a good idea to bring in our CEO.

"'You can do it if you wish,' the group's representative replied. 'We're sure our CEO would be delighted to visit with yours. But it won't do you any good. We're an empowered team, and we have the full authority to make the decision about whom to give this contract to.'

"So," continued Cardenas, "our team debated the matter and decided not to bring in our CEO. They told his office he need not come."

Susan and Charles were wide-eyed. "They told the CEO not to come?" Charles asked in disbelief.

"Yes," Cardenas nodded, grinning.

"That was taking one heck of a risk," Charles remarked.

"It certainly was," Cardenas responded. "But the team had decided that if they didn't bring in our CEO and every other competitor did, it might give us a small degree of distinction."

Charles shook his head, still amazed at the team's decision to rebuff the firm's CEO.

"At least it worked out well for them," Cardenas concluded. "We learned just this morning that we've received the contract. It's a huge one and we're all delighted."

He reached for a folder on his desk. "I wish it were my achievement too," he mused, "but the team doesn't report to me. I do supervise some of the team's members, but it also has members who work for other bosses. So the team really is its own boss. And they did a good job."

He stopped and thought for a moment. "Maybe too good a job," he said with a wry smile. "Now they'll want a big bonus for their success, and then they'll want us to find them another opportunity like this, so they can have a chance to hit another homer and win another big bonus."

As he got up from his desk, he added, "I really won't be having much time for you. With the delayering, I now have far too many people reporting to me for me to spend much time with any one or two of them. And I have these cross-functional teams to work with. You're going to be on your own to a much greater degree than in the past. But I have confidence in each of you and know you'll do a good job."

With the folder tucked under his arm, he hurried toward his office door. "You can stay here until you're finished meeting," he called back to them before bounding out the door and down the hall.

The office was quiet for a few moments. Finally, Charles broke the silence by asking the obvious question: "What are we going to do, Susan?"

"I don't know," she replied. "I'm already working as fast as I can. If we keep going like this—downsizing and trying to do as much as before—we'll just run ourselves to death."

"What alternative do we have?" Charles asked her.

"We could try something different."

"Whatever we do," he suggested, "I think we ought to play to win, not just to keep from losing."

"Yes, I agree," Susan responded. "We're already losing just by trying not to lose. Also, I think we should try to love preparing to win. What we've really got to do is find a way to transform this company into a winner. We've got to keep our costs down, get our quality up, and be so responsive to customers that we blow away our competition. Then we can stop downsizing all the time. I'm sick of laying off people."

"It's all up there on the board," Charles said, gesturing toward the white board with the list Cardenas had written on it. "See? Cost, quality, and responsiveness."

"Yes," Susan said pensively, "it's all there, except . . ."

She stood up and walked over to the white board. On it she added, as the final outcome of what John Cardenas had written previously:

- *A New Management Style*

- *A New Organization Structure*

She turned to Charles, who shook his head in agreement. Then he went over to the white board and accepted the marker which she offered him.

"We could try using empowered teams, like the one that just won that big contract," he suggested. Turning to the board he wrote opposite what Susan had written:

- *A New Management Style–EMPOWERMENT*

- *A New Organization Structure–*
  Empowered Teams

"But if we agree to try this, we have to understand what it really means," Charles continued.

"Yes," Susan replied.

"We ought to set up a program with goals and timetables," he proposed.

But Susan frowned upon hearing this. "You engineers," she said. "You always want to make a program of everything. You'll overmanage it to death."

"If you can't measure it, you can't manage it," Charles said with certainty.

He went to write on the board, then hesitated. "What exactly are we talking about anyway? What is an empowered team? How does it work? Are you and I supposed to be part of it? How will we supervise it?"

"I think we can just do it," Susan suggested. "We don't need to make a big deal out of it. We'll just set up some teams and tell people that now they're to make the decisions and take action."

9

The look of astonishment on Charles' face made her reluctant to say anything more. The two colleagues looked at each other for a few moments in silence, until Susan gave in.

"I think," she said, "that some people can accept a new way of working without needing extensive preparation. They can be fully flexible—just let things go the new way. But others need a framework—a concept—to provide them with an understanding of what the new method is, of what they're expected to do and how different it is from the way they worked in the past."

"I need that," Charles said, "and the people who work for me need it too."

"So we have to offer a framework," Susan concluded.

"Let's work up a set of goals for our effort," Charles suggested.

After an hour at the white board, the two had worked out a list of objectives:

Goals for Organizational Transformation

To meet our goals, we will do the following:

1. Learn a common academic model of management
2. Improve our understanding of the reasons for the shift in management styles
3. Develop a common understanding of empowerment
4. Introduce empowered teams
5. Add to our efforts to transform the business
6. Obtain converts for the transformation effort
7. Reinforce the company's continuous quality-improvement effort
8. Build for the long term while improving immediate performance

"If we get all this done," Susan said, "it will help people to understand the concept of empowerment and to see how it applies to us. It will also help us get comfortable with it."

"It's our only hope," Charles said. "Otherwise we'll be spinning in circles, trying to supervise everything that needs to be done. We have to do this without help from our boss and with fewer and fewer people and a shrinking budget."

"Yes," Susan agreed. "We must *never try to solve the management problem of the Nineties with the management style of the past.*"

At the conclusion of their discussion, Charles went to the board and summarized their thoughts as follows:

- **Increased Competition**
  More Rapid Change ⟶ **yield the need for**

- **Reduced Cost**
  Improved Quality
  Enhanced Responsiveness ⟶ **which leads to**

- **Downsizing**
  Delayering
  Total Quality Management
  Market-Driven Quality
  Increased Delegation
  Cross-Functional Teams ⟶ **which have created**

- **A New Management Style**
  A New Organization
      Structure ⟶ **which are**

- **A New Management Style—EMPOWERMENT**
  A New Organization Structure—
      Empowered Teams

REMEMBER: Never try to solve the management problem of the Nineties with the management style of the past.

Chapter 2

A Better Way of Working

Early the next week Charles received a note from John Cardenas. It explained that Cardenas was going to the Middle East for two weeks, where he would be very busy and unable to be reached. It also informed Charles that his company had just learned of an opportunity that needed to be seized. Word had been received by corporate headquarters that Appex Corporation was ready to sell a business unit that Charles' company had been anxious to acquire for some time. The note instructed Charles to go to Milwaukee immediately to see Ron Jackson, Appex's attorney, to try to make a deal for the acquisition.

After phoning his travel agent to reserve airline tickets, Charles went down the hall to his assistant's office to get Ron Jackson's phone number. He wanted to call the attorney for an appointment.

His assistant, Haley Lendoff, listened to his request for Jackson's number.

"Why do you need it?" she asked.

Normally Charles would have responded, "What difference does that make? You don't need to know why I need it. Just give it to me now, I'm in a hurry!" This time he thought better of it, though. He knew he should take a minute to answer Haley's question or Haley wouldn't buy into the request. This is what participative management is all about, Charles reminded himself. So, exercising a little patience, he related to Haley the message he had received from Cardenas.

"That's strange," Haley responded.

"What do you mean 'strange'?" Charles asked in surprise.

"The word I have is that Appex may sell—that part's right—but it's not Ron Jackson who's the key player on their side; it's Philip Kowalski."

"Kowalski?" Charles asked. "In Houston?"

"Yes, in Houston."

"How do you know?"

"Well, one of my good friends from college works for Appex, and I told him about our interest in that division. Our competitors are also interested, you know, so I asked him to be sure to keep me up to date on what's going on about it. He told me they're looking to sell very quickly and that Philip Kowalski is the key decision-maker."

Charles looked at his assistant quizzically. "Why would your friend's information be more accurate than the information John has?"

"Well," Haley said cautiously, "there's more to the story. My friend is with the division, and he thinks that if we buy it, I'll help him keep his job, so he's very anxious to help us make the acquisition. Also, there's been a big power struggle underway in Appex. Ron Jackson is Philip Kowalski's superior, but Philip is moving up very fast. He's now the chairman's favorite, and it's likely he'll be promoted over Jackson next year. He's getting all the key assignments, but because Jackson is very sensitive about the issue, the company is maintaining the outward appearance that Jackson's still in charge. In other words, Cardenas has the official story—yes, Appex's division is for sale fast, and yes, Ron Jackson is formally in charge of the sale. But the unofficial, accurate story is that the division is for sale immediately and that Philip Kowalski is going to decide whom it's sold to."

"You're sure about this?" Charles asked intently.

"Absolutely. In fact, I was going to come see you about this in just a few minutes. My friend called me this morning to tell me the story and to say that one of our competitors is already on Kowalski's calendar. He wanted us to send a representative to Houston immediately."

"What if I go to Milwaukee first?"

"You'll probably lose the deal. Ron Jackson will play like he's the guy to make the decision, so he won't refer you to Kowalski, but he'll have to go to Kowalski himself for approval. That'll take a long time and probably won't work too well, since Jackson and Kowalski are rivals. No, I think if you go to Milwaukee instead of Houston, you can kiss the deal good-bye."

Charles shook his head in indecision and told Haley he'd be back to her later.

Upon returning to his office, he found Susan waiting for him, ready to pick up where they'd left off last week in John Cardenas' office. As he mind was too full of the Appex matter for him to give attention to anything else, he asked Susan if he could discuss the matter with her.

She was happy to help him out, so Charles described the instruction he had received from Cardenas and what his assistant had said about it.

"You can't see both Jackson and Kowalski?" Susan asked.

"Not in any way I can figure out," Charles said. "If I see Jackson, I'll lose out on making a deal with Kowalski. If I see Kowalski, Jackson will be angry with me. But if Haley Lendoff is right, I suppose it doesn't matter if Jackson is angry at me, as Kowalski is the key guy."

"And you can't reach John?"

"He's en route to the Mideast, and even if I could, he's busy with other things. He's already told me what he wants me to do."

"Not exactly," Susan objected. "He's told you to do two things—two different, even inconsistent, things."

"Well," Charles said, "they weren't inconsistent in his mind. He said to sign the Appex deal and to see Jackson, and he thought Jackson was the key to the Appex deal."

"Yes, but now you have unofficial information that suggests that may not be the case, right?" Susan asked.

"Right."

"So what should you do?"

"You tell me."

"All right," Susan agreed, accepting the challenge, "let's think about it. What are the reasons for doing what John says to do—going to Milwaukee to see Jackson?"

15

"Well," Charles offered, "maybe he's right. Maybe Jackson is in charge of the deal. He said he has his information from corporate headquarters."

"Do you think corporate headquarters is more likely to be accurate than Haley Lendoff's friend in Appex?" Susan asked.

Charles snorted cynically. "Are you kidding? Of course not."

Susan went over to a flip chart that stood in a corner of his office and wrote on it the following heading:

Reasons to Follow Orders

Under that heading, she wrote:

• *Headquarters might be right.*

After looking over her work, she turned to Charles and said, "But Appex could have given the assignment to Kowalski and then have changed its mind and given it to Jackson. In which case, you'd be okay in going to Milwaukee."

"That's wishful thinking," Charles objected. "It'd be quite a coincidence if that happened. I wouldn't want to bet on it."

He thought about the problem as Susan added to her list:

• *Customer might have changed its mind.*

"There's the chance that I might only be part of a plan," he speculated. "Maybe someone else is being sent to see Kowalski. Then if I disregarded John's instructions and went to Houston, I might disrupt the plan. Furthermore, John thinks I'll be in Milwaukee. If he wants me, that's where he'll look for me. If I go to Houston, he won't know where I am. If everyone in our organization disregarded orders and just did what he or she thought was right, we'd have chaos, anarchy!"

His outburst made Susan smile broadly as she wrote:

• *I'm part of a plan.*

"You know," she said, "it occurs to me that what we're discussing is a classic case of precisely what we were talking about last week in John's office. Think about it. The boss has gone off and left an instruction, but you have knowledge that suggests the instruction is wrong. The question is, Do you act on your own initiative or not? Do you use your own discretion or not? Last week we were discussing empowerment. This is a question about empowerment. Are you empowered to act as you see fit, or must you adhere narrowly to instructions?"

Charles listened to her thoughtfully.

Susan continued: "I think that if John had asked you to go to Milwaukee as only part of a larger plan to make that acquisition, he'd have let you know about it. At least, he should have let you know about it. His instructions told you to make the deal. If there'd been other people in the plan, I don't think he'd have put it that way. In other words, the instruction itself implies that there's no larger plan.

"As for his not knowing where you are, you can just leave a message for him that you're in Houston, and if he calls looking for you, he'll get the message."

"But there are still two other reasons why I probably should do what the orders told me to do," Charles said.

"What are they?" Susan asked.

"First, that's what's expected of me. In our company, we're expected to obey our superiors' instructions. That why we each have a boss, why there's a chain of command. If I don't do what I'm told, then I'm setting an example of disobedience for the people who work for me. What if they ignore my instructions?"

Susan smiled again. "Don't be so uptight," she said. "If you left an instruction for Haley and she knew a better way to accomplish the objective, what would you want her to do?"

"Get the objective done," Charles admitted.

"So there," Susan concluded. She added to her list:

- *It's what's expected of me.*

"There's still one last issue," Charles told her.

"I think I know what it is," she replied. "It's the issue of your career, right? There's a career calculation involved."

Charles nodded.

Susan wrote at the bottom of her list:

- *I must protect my career.*

"What if Haley's wrong?" Charles asked. "Or what if I go to Houston and can't sign Kowalski to the deal? In that case, I've both failed to get the deal and disobeyed John's direct instruction to go to Milwaukee."

"Actually," Susan said, "there are four possible outcomes. First, you go to Milwaukee and you sign the deal. That's very good."

Charles smiled in agreement.

"Second," she continued, "you go to Milwaukee and you don't sign the deal. That's not great, but it's not your fault. You didn't know that Jackson wasn't the key guy. You just followed orders, and if it didn't work out, it's John's responsibility, not yours."

"Right," Charles concurred

"Third," Susan went on, "you go to Houston and you sign the deal. That's good, though some bosses might get angry even about that."

"Yes," Charles agreed. "In college our coach once told our quarterback to pass. Instead, he ran the ball for a game-winning touchdown. The coach thanked him for the victory, but made him run laps as punishment for disobeying instructions."

"I don't think John would be like that," Susan said.

"I hope not."

"Fourth," she said, resuming her list, "you go to Houston and you don't make the deal. That is very bad. Not only have you failed to make the acquisition, but you've disobeyed John's instructions to go to Milwaukee. You could be in deep trouble. Your career could be seriously set back, right?"

"That's what's troubling me," Charles said.

"Well," Susan replied, "that's a tough one. Let's look for a moment at the reasons to go to Houston, as Haley recommends."

She paused for thought, then said, "A very good reason might be that the mission is to make the deal to buy the Appex division . . ."

"And going to Houston is the most likely way to accomplish that," Charles added, completing her idea.

Susan wrote on the other side of the same sheet of flip-chart paper:

Reasons to Use My Own Discretion

Under this heading, she noted first:

- *Best way to accomplish the mission*

"Also," said Charles, "Haley probably has the most accurate, up-to-date, from-the-site information."

Susan wrote:

- *Best information*

"Do you have confidence in Haley?" Susan asked.

"Yes," Charles answered promptly. "She's well trained, experienced, and reliable. She's very likely to be right about what to do."

Susan added to her list:

- *Competent advisor*

Charles studied both lists that Susan had written. "I think," he said, "that what I'm really expected to do is make an effort to accomplish the objective, not just follow orders. So you can put 'It's what's expected of me' on both sides."

Susan did, writing:

- *It's what's expected of me*

"That's a strong list," she said after regarding it carefully. She walked away from the flip chart and sat down again. "But it doesn't address one key issue: the question of what's best for your career."

"I noticed that," Charles said ruefully.

"Let's put that one off for just a while," Susan suggested. "At this point—without considering the effect on your career if you do what Haley suggests and it doesn't work out—what conclusion would you reach?"

Charles answered without hesitation, "I'd do what Haley suggests."

"I thought so," Susan responded. "You'd act in an empowered fashion, using your own judgment to accomplish the mission. You wouldn't simply follow orders."

She glanced back at the flip chart, then looked at Charles. "You know, in talking with you like this it occurs to me that if we step back mentally and consider the process we've just been through, it may have a lot to teach us about the broader question of empowerment that we've been discussing. This Appex question has been kind of an example of the broader issue, a case in point."

"What do you want to do?" Charles asked her.

"Let's suppose that your decision—to go where Haley suggests—is the right one. Let's ask ourselves what conditions are necessary for it to be the right one."

"That's easy," replied Charles. "I sign the Appex deal."

"That's a very strong condition," Susan laughed. "If it's really applicable, then you'd never act on your own initiative unless you were virtually certain in advance that the action would turn out exactly as planned. And few things do. So if that were a condition, very little would ever be done in an empowered fashion."

"That's right," Charles admitted.

"I mean more reasonable conditions," Susan said. "For example, that you had confidence in Haley's competence."

"Yes," Charles agreed. "Also, that I had the necessary information to make the decision."

Susan went back to the flip chart and turned up a clean sheet of paper. At its top, she wrote:

Conditions for Empowerment

Under the heading, she wrote:

- *Competence and experience*

- *Necessary information*

"And I should be rewarded if I take the risk of using my own judgment and it works out, shouldn't I?" Charles asked. "Otherwise, I wouldn't be likely to bother, would I? I'd just follow orders blindly."

"Yes, I think you would," Susan said, teasing him. "Actually, that's a great point. I remember a term that was supposedly coined at Ford Motor Company: *malicious obedience*. It refers to when a subordinate carries out the instruction of a supervisor to the letter even though the subordinate knows the instruction is a mistake and can harm the company."

"As if I were to follow the directive to go to Milwaukee even though I knew that Houston was the place where something could be accomplished?" Charles asked.

"Yes," Susan replied. "That would be malicious obedience."

She added to her list:

- *A proper reward*

They both thought for a minute.

Suddenly Susan's face lit up. "There's one that's critical, but it's so obvious we've been missing it," she said excitedly.

"What?" Charles asked.

"The mission—the objective," she responded. "We must know the mission. If the objective isn't to make that deal, then it's a great mistake to go to Houston as Haley suggests."

"But why—?" Charles began.

"Oh, I don't know," Susan interrupted, quickly grasping the question. "John might have wanted you to go to Milwaukee for some reason he wasn't prepared to tell you about, using the Appex acquisition as a subterfuge to get you to go. But anyway, I'm not suggesting that's the case here, only that if we didn't have the mission right, then using our discretion in determining how to accomplish it would almost certainly be the wrong thing to do."

"You're right," Charles agreed. "Actually, I think that may happen often. Managers aren't very good at developing clear objectives for people—either because they don't themselves know what the people ought to be doing, or because they can't express it well. We usually just give people narrow tasks to accomplish, not objectives to fulfill."

"Exactly!" Susan exclaimed. "Having the mission right is crucial, but it's not easy to do."

She added to her list:

• *Must know the mission*

"That's a good list," Charles commented. "It needs only one more thing."

"What?"

"If I'm to use my discretion to accomplish a mission, then I must have confidence that if it doesn't work out, I won't lose my career; otherwise, the risk will usually be too high."

"I know," Susan said. "I'd like to have a nickel for every management meeting I've been in lately in which our executives exhort us to take more risks. 'You've got to act quicker, to take more risks,' they say. 'The business world is moving faster and we have to move quicker to keep up with it.'

"Then we go out in the hall for a coffee break," she continued, "and I hear one person turn to another and whisper, 'Sure, take a risk, and the first time it turns out wrong, your career is over.'"

"That's the career calculation back again," Charles pointed out.

Susan agreed. "There must be some fault tolerance in the system. Some mistakes must be okay; if they're not, most people won't take risks with their careers."

She added to the bottom of the list:

• *Fault tolerance*

Then she stepped back and looked at the flip chart. "I think we've made a lot of progress," she said proudly.

"Yes," Charles said, "we have. So there they are: five critical conditions that make delegation or empowerment possible. I think these conditions are at the heart of what we were discussing last week."

"There is one more thing we could ask ourselves," Susan suddenly suggested. "I think this is kind of an extra-credit question on the exam we've been giving ourselves."

"What is it?"

"If you could communicate with John now, would you?"

"But I can't—you know that," Chalres protested. "He said I couldn't reach him."

"Yes, but suppose you could. Would you?"

"Of course I would. What a silly question."

"Maybe it's not so silly," Susan said. "What would you say to him?"

"I'd say, 'Here's what Haley told me. What should I do?'"

"Suppose it took you a while to reach him," Susan said. "Or suppose you left that message for him. Would you wait for him to reply?"

"Well, no. I might just leave the message that I was going to Houston, so that he would know where I was if he needed me."

"I think that's the right answer," Susan said, "because you already know what your mission is—to make the acquisition deal—and you know how to do it because Haley has given you good information, even better than what John has. So why do you need to hear from him? You don't. If you contact him and wait for instructions, what you're really doing is trying to shift the responsibility for a decision back to him—you just want to carry out an order—and rejecting the empowerment. But if you leave a message with information, then you're helping him and getting on with the mission. That's the right thing to do."

Charles thought about Susan's point for a long moment. Now he saw what empowerment was really about. It was about accepting a higher degree of responsibility for his own actions. He was no longer accountable only for carrying out an order; now he was accountable for a decision and its consequences. It was much riskier. He suddenly realized why some of his own people might be hesitant about accepting empowerment.

One last time Susan went over to the flip chart. She threw back the last sheet of paper she'd filled and on a new sheet wrote:

Never empower people when they
- *don't know the mission*
- *don't have the necessary information*
- *don't have the necessary competence*
- *are afraid to take action*

Both Susan and Charles felt that they had truly accomplished something at their meeting. After Susan left his office, Charles again looked over what they had written on the flip chart:

Reasons to Follow Orders
- *Headquarters might be right.*
- *Customer might have changed its mind.*
- *I'm part of a plan.*
- *It's what's expected of me.*
- *I must protect my career.*

Reasons to Use Own Discretion
- *Best way to accomplish the objective*
- *Best information*
- *Competent advisor*
- *It's what's expected of me.*

Conditions for Empowerment
- *Competence and experience*
- *Necessary information*
- *A proper reward*
- *Must know the mission*
- *Fault tolerance*

Never empower people when they
- *don't know the mission*
- *don't have the necessary information*
- *don't have the necessary competence*
- *are afraid to take action*

Chapter 3

The Three Management Styles

To Susan's surprise, she received from Charles an invitation to a meeting in the conference room the day after they had talked in his office.

"I thought you'd be in Houston," she told him when she entered the conference room and found Charles waiting.

"Philip Kowalski postponed our meeting until next week," he briefly explained, "so I thought we should keep going with our discussions about transforming our organization."

"Good," Susan said. "But why are we meeting here? Is someone else coming?"

"I've invited Doug Royal from the corporate staff," Charles replied. "He's had some experience with these things, and we've talked about similar issues before. Have you met him?"

"No."

"He's been with the company for two years. Before that he was with several other big firms. He's seen efforts to transform a company succeed, and he's seen them fail. Now he's an internal consultant for us. I've often listened to him speak about these matters, and rather than trying to repeat what I've heard, I thought it'd be better if I arranged a meeting so that you could hear him for yourself. I think he's very good."

Susan nodded.

Soon a tall, graying man entered the room and introduced himself to her. He was Doug Royal.

Charles described to Doug what he and Susan had been doing. He had the flip-chart sheets on which Susan had recorded the lists she and Charles had produced, and as he taped them along the wall, he asked Susan to explain the rationale behind the lists to Doug. She did so.

"We think we understand the conditions for empowerment," Susan told Doug, "but we're unclear what it's actually about. When are we empowering people and when aren't we? What is it we're trying to do?"

Doug smiled as she finished. "I find a lot of people are confused about this," he responded. "I have a way of thinking about it that I'll share with you. I already talked with Charles once before about it."

"Yes, and it was very helpful," Charles said. "That's why I asked you to join us, so you could repeat it."

"But you've already heard it," Doug protested. "You don't want to go through it again."

"Yes, I do," Charles insisted. He paused, then added: "You know, I remember a college professor of mine years ago. He told me that every year he would give a summary lecture at the start of the term and repeat the same lecture, verbatim, at the end of the term. After hearing his final lecture, students would come to him and ask, 'Why didn't you tell us that at the start of the term?' He'd reply, 'I did, but that was before you'd been through the coursework, and you didn't have enough knowledge to understand it then.'"

Charles continued: "I feel like that about what you have to say. I've heard it before, but I really haven't fully understood it. Now that I've been talking about it with Susan and experimenting with it in an assignment I have from my boss, I have more background, and I think if I listen to you again, I'll have a much deeper understanding."

Doug smiled in response, very pleased with Charles' attitude. He took a place near the electronic board and began to speak.

"What we have here," he said, "is a new management style. The best way to understand it is to contrast it with the two styles that preceded it and now coexist with it.

"There's a formulation of what defines management that gained currency in the 1930s and that provides a powerful but simple picture of the difference between the traditional and the new styles."

Doug stood up and went to the board.

"What managers do, the traditional formulation says, is organize, deputize, and supervise."

He wrote on the board:

Organize
Deputize
Supervise

"First, a manager or an executive—the boss—decides what is to be done and how to split the tasks up among the different people or units of the firm; that is, he or she organizes. Then the boss decides whom to make responsible for getting certain things done and assigns them clear, individual responsibility; that is, he or she deputizes. Finally, the boss—or others selected by the boss—supervises carefully to ensure that people complete their assignments on time and properly.

"This is the traditional system of management. We'll label it 'ODS' for Organize/Deputize/Supervise. It's a highly directive system of management: The boss gives instructions and the subordinate carries them out."

He added to what he'd written on the board until it read:

Traditional Management

Directive

ODS (A)   *ODS (B)*

Organize
Deputize
Supervise

"You'll note," Doug said, "that I've listed two forms of ODS: ODS (A) and ODS (B). This is because traditional, directive management can be done in either of two ways: autocratically or participatively. The autocratic executive makes all decisions independently, without consulting others. The participative executive solicits the opinions of subordinates when making decisions about what to do, how to organize work, whom to assign tasks to, and even how and when to supervise."

Charles, who was a history buff, interjected at this point, "I know the classic example of an autocrat."

"Who?" Doug asked.

"Otto von Bismarck, the nineteenth-century German chancellor," he replied. "When asked how he made the decision to go to war with France as a way to establish the German empire, he answered, 'I thought the matter out in solitary communion with God and did not consult the members of my party.'"

"Perfect!" Doug exclaimed, smiling broadly. "And there are a lot of executives like that also."

"Yes," Charles and Susan agreed simultaneously.

"Let me summarize," Doug suggested. "The traditional system—whether done in an autocratic or a participative fashion—is directive; that is, subordinates are told what to do. They may be told without being given an opportunity to provide any input—autocratically—or they may be told after having provided input—participatively—but in either situation, they are told. They carry out orders. In the past many middle managers made a shibboleth of order taking. 'What we're proud of,' they'd say, 'is our ability to get things done. You tell us what to do—give us the task—and we'll carry it out brilliantly. But don't ask us to participate in the decisions. Just give us clear direction.' This was the attitude that won World War II. The 'can do' attitude.

"It was a very effective management system when it was at its peak. But in the 1960s and 1970s, business grew more complicated and people's attitudes changed. They began to mistrust those in authority and to demand more involvement in their work. Being consulted by one's boss before receiving orders came to be expected to such a degree that if employees weren't consulted, they didn't really feel that they owed much commitment. Today, for example, if your boss were to make a decision that would have a major impact on your department, but didn't discuss it with you in advance, would you feel an obligation to carry out the decision to the best of your ability?"

Susan and Charles sat thinking.

Doug explained, "I mean, you'd do it well enough not to get fired, but you wouldn't really buy into it or have your heart in it."

"Yes, you're right," Susan said. "If I weren't consulted, I wouldn't have my heart in it."

"I agree," added Charles. "Unless I were consulted, I wouldn't feel any moral obligation to carry out the decision to the best of my ability. I wouldn't have been treated fairly."

"There you have it," said Doug. "That's the source of the participative management revolution. Key employees began to insist that unless they were allowed to participate in decisions, they wouldn't buy into them, and without buy-in, a company couldn't get the commitment it needed from key employees in order to be successful. So companies began to adopt a more participative form of management. That's where its source lay—in the changing expectations and aspirations of people. Companies didn't start participative management out of their own good hearts. If people hadn't demanded different treatment, we'd still have only autocratic management.

"But they did demand involvement, so we have ODS autocratic and ODS participative—the traditional and directive management styles. It's one or the other of these two styles that most people have in mind when they talk about management. These traditional styles are what management gurus mean when they say 'Managers must manage'—that is, must organize, deputize, and supervise.

"Until a few years ago, ODS in its two forms was all there was to say about how people were managed. But now a new style has emerged, and it's rapidly becoming popular. It's a wholly different style, a third form.

"We know it's a truly new form because it differs from ODS in every particular. In place of deciding what's to be done and organizing the tasks, a manager establishes goals for an individual or a team; in place of deputizing individuals or departments to carry out certain tasks, the manager empowers them to accomplish the goals in the manner they see best, utilizing the resources at their disposal; and in place of supervising to see that the tasks are done correctly and on schedule, the manager measures the results to see if the goals are accomplished. It is, if you will, an extreme form of management by delegation."

Doug turned to the electronic board and wrote opposite the Traditional Management list:

New

Set Goals
Empower
Measure

"This," said Doug, "is the GEM style of management. It is sometimes referred to simply as empowerment." He added several final touches to his board. "Thus we have three styles of management, as the table on the board indicates."

He stepped to one side so that Susan and Charles could clearly see what he had written.

Styles of Management

Traditional	*New*
ODS	*GEM*
1. Autocratic 2. Participative *(ODS – A) (ODS – P)*	*3. Empowering*
Organize *Deputize* *Supervise*	*Set Goals* *Empower* *Measure*

"Once we recognize that there are now three management styles, not two, then certain key conclusions become apparent. First, this table makes clear that the new style, GEM, is not participative management. It isn't that GEM isn't participative—it is—but it goes much further in many respects than traditional participative management. GEM is something much more dramatic than ODS (P).

"There is great confusion about this in business, government, and the media. The confusion arises from the misconception that empowering is no more than traditional participative management. It is much more than that. Empowering involves giving people freedom that goes far beyond the consultation which is at the heart of participative management."

Susan turned her attention from the electronic board to Doug.

"I think," she said, "that in our division we've been moving from autocratic management to participative management, all the while believing that what we were doing was empowering people. No wonder everyone around here is so confused. We haven't understood what we've been doing. We've told people that we're empowering them when all we've really done is let them participate a bit more. We thought we were making big progress, but in reality, we haven't gone very far at all."

She shook her head in disappointment; then she said to Doug, "This is very helpful, to understand what we've really been doing."

"But I still don't understand completely how participation differs from empowerment," Charles said to both Susan and Doug.

"I think you can only grasp it through repeated examples," Doug said. "Here's one of the differences between a participative management response and one that expresses the new idea of an empowered action.

"Several middle managers received a directive from top management requiring the termination of a portion of the workforce, which would be selected according to the employees' performance levels. It was to be the first layoff in the company's history.

"Most managers approached the matter by getting their group of immediate subordinates together to decide how to identify poor performers. They were trying to carry out the directive within their own departments in a participative style by involving their subordinates. Also, each department was choosing its own course of action to carry out the assignment. This was a directive participative management approach.

"But one manager suggested that this major reduction in force was intended to change the company's culture from one of employment security to one of reward for performance. To be sure that departments acted consistently with one other—thereby establishing a new corporate culture—he proposed to begin by meeting with his peers from other departments to decide on a common course of action. If they could not all agree to the same procedure, they would go to higher management for the resolution of the dispute.

"This was an empowered response. Why? Because the manager looked at the instructions he'd received as goals and sought to address the matter in an imaginative way. The imaginative manager saw himself as part of an empowered team of his peers, a team who should try to accomplish the goals in the way that would produce the best results for the company. He was trying to do what his superiors wanted him to do, not simply what they told him to do. The others simply started to carry out their orders, even though they were trying to do it in a participative way. They didn't perceive themselves as part of a team or as broadly empowered, although they surely thought of themselves, correctly, as participative managers.

"Realizing that there are three management styles," Doug continued, "also makes evident another important aspect of empowering. Empowerment is not real for people, and not wise for a company, unless it is sandwiched between goals and measurement. People can't pursue a goal unless they know what it is, and a company dare not send people out on their own accord without any clear purpose. If people are clear about their goals and are empowered, then they are likely to act, and the result can only be what the company intended by accident. So empowerment has to be coupled with goals.

"Furthermore, an executive cannot determine who has been successfully empowered and reward them appropriately unless the progress of each person or team can be measured in relation to its goals. If it can't be, then people who accomplish their goals can't be distinguished from those who don't. People will see the wrong individuals getting rewarded and will be demoralized and quit taking action."

"This," Susan interrupted to say to Charles, "tracks exactly what we were saying when we discussed the conditions for empowerment."

Charles agreed.

"So empowerment in the workplace," Doug continued, "must be coupled with both goals and measurement; otherwise, it will not work. There is no such thing as empowerment outside the GEM style—because there can't be real empowerment without goals and measurement.

"Some people prefer to think of the goals that are provided to empowered teams or individuals as elements of a mission. That's the way the military would put it. A mission is a clearly defined short- or intermediate-term objective or set of objectives established for an individual, a team, or a larger organizational unit. Please note that the term *mission* as I'm using it here means something quite different from a general mission statement of the overall purpose of a firm or division, nor is it a corporate or departmental vision. Establishing proper missions is a crucial task of executives."

"I'm not sure I fully understand that," Susan said. "It seems to me that *mission* and *mission statement* and *vision* are all mixed up in one big morass of jargon."

"That's a little strong," Doug responded, "but you have a point. Terminology, however helpful it can be, is often overwhelming. There is as much confusion over the difference between those terms as there is over the difference between *empowerment* and *participation*.

"Briefly, a *vision* is a goal that appears impossible to actually accomplish. It's rooted in imagination and foresight, and fostered by the belief that, against all odds, its challenge can be met. NASA's vision in the early 1960s of putting a man on the moon is one example of such a goal. A vision is a helpful leadership device whatever management style is being used. A *mission statement* is a set of values for an organization. It's a list of the things we hold dear. Finally, a *mission*—as in GEM—is a short- or intermediate-term objective that is specific and measurable, and so serves as the basis for the delegation of responsibility to an individual or a team. It's much broader than a task, but not as broad as a vision. It's an operational concept.

"I think we should return to this topic at a later date," he concluded. "We'll spend more time on it then, because establishing proper missions or goals is a crucial element of GEM management."

"Or maybe Charles and I will be able to figure it out for ourselves," Susan added.

"Maybe," Charles agreed.

"I want to emphasize," Doug said, "that despite all the discussion about the differences between autocratic and participative management, the two ODS styles are very much alike. Organizations regularly move back and forth along the continuum between them. Whenever a new executive comes in, everyone assesses his or her leadership style—how participative he or she is—and adapts accordingly. People adapt, but personnel systems don't have to change; basic attitudes and work methods don't have to change.

"In contrast, GEM isn't readily consistent with the traditional styles. To change from GEM to ODS, people in an organization must make big changes in attitudes, behaviors, and even policies and practices—changes which are difficult to accomplish and can't easily be reversed. That's very strong evidence that GEM is a truly different management style from the traditional systems."

"One thing I don't understand," Charles said, "is how you know which style fits best in a given situation. Take our situation, for example. Should we be trying to go to GEM, or should we be satisfied with participative management?"

"I think empowerment is best in any situation," Susan responded. "It frees people to do their best."

"We disagree there," Doug said. "I don't think any of the three styles is clearly best for all situations. ODS has worked well for centuries and is what most people mean by management. It has a big advantage in that people are familiar with it. But ODS has two big limitations: it's slow—due to the many levels of review before a decision is made and an action taken—and it's expensive—due to the many levels of management and supervision involved. In effect, ODS is a very bureaucratic form of management, and consequently, it's expensive.

"In the past, slow and expensive management systems were often acceptable. When a firm had large market share, good margins, and a slow rate of change, it could afford to have a bureaucracy that gave top executives the feeling of tight control and that made decisions only when the firm was certain they were right and it could go ahead with them.

"But for many firms, including ours, this is no longer the situation. Now we face rapid change and intense competition. Being slow and expensive is a fatal flaw in the ODS system."

"I have a friend who works for a large company," Susan said. "The other day she told me about the difficulties her company is having. 'We were so successful for so long,' she said. 'We thought it was because we were great managers and studied everything until we got it just right. Now we're in deep trouble, and we're beginning to think our earlier success was only due to the fact we had a monopoly.'"

"That's exactly the point," Doug said. "What we had identified as great management was really only a bureaucratic procedure to minimize risk while we were reaping the rewards of little competition and a stable environment. When those things changed, our traditional management style was revealed to be wanting."

The three sat quietly for a few moments. Doug rested. Susan and Charles thought.

Charles broke the silence. "Is GEM the Japanese management style?" he asked.

"No," Doug replied. "The Japanese system is essentially traditional participative management. The Japanese didn't invent the system, but they've gone a long way toward perfecting it. They've developed many imaginative mechanisms for employee participation—including consensus management, quality circles, and continuous improvement—but they still use lots of supervision. For example, the typical large Japanese manufacturing plant has six or seven levels of management, just as plants in Europe and America do. And while the Japanese use teams, they don't empower them. Japanese employees work under close supervision. Also, a quality circle isn't an empowered team—it's a meeting in which supervisors and workers try to resolve production problems. It gives workers a voice in the company, but the supervisors still direct the work.

"No, empowering isn't a Japanese thing. When Japanese executives study empowered teams in American companies, they say, 'It's very interesting, but we don't go that far.' Instead, GEM is largely a western development, a means by which American and European firms are attempting to reach the levels of success enjoyed by Japanese firms.

"American firms have at their disposal neither a work ethic like that of Japanese employees nor a government as supportive as that of Japan. For a great many reasons, the work ethic in the traditional American business setting is not competitive, and the support of the American government for business is often lukewarm or inadequate. To offset these disadvantages, our firms are trying to develop a new style of management that can be combined with new technology and new products to provide costs, customer responsiveness, quality, and productivity that match or exceed Japanese standards.

"That's the broad perspective on what GEM is and why it's been developing," Doug concluded his explanation.

"Are any Japanese firms using GEM?" Charles asked. "If it's such a good thing, they would adopt it, wouldn't they?"

"Some are beginning to use GEM," Doug answered. "The delayered organization and management by delegation to empowered teams have been closely observed by some Japanese firms. In 1992 enough progress had been made in the west that Toyota embarked on its own efforts to achieve the higher productivity and lower costs that GEM promises. Every Toyota plant, in Japan as well as in the United States, is undergoing a transition from ODS-P to GEM, from seven levels of management and supervision at the plant level to two: plant manager and team leader. If empowerment can work for western firms, Toyota apparently believes that it can work for Japanese firms as well."

After Doug finished there was another lengthy pause. Then Susan offered a personal observation, leading the discussion into a new area of thought.

"I think of GEM as more than just a management style," Susan said. "I see it as a change in the very way the individual relates to work. I think the key to the explosive strength of empowerment for improving a person's life and work performance lies in fitting his or her work and personal life into a larger context. At the deepest level, empowerment reflects a different way of relating to others and to oneself—a way of being positive about life, of rejecting the disillusionment that happens and that so often becomes a rationale for bitterness and withdrawal. Since the contest between a positive attitude and a negative one occurs in both a person's personal life and business life, empowerment occurs in both aspects of a person's life too. It finds opportunity in the world around us and strives to be free to seize it. In business, freedom is limited by a person's supervisor; in private life, by the scars a person bears from having gone through bad experiences. When a person is freed of these limitations, he or she is empowered."

Energized by her own eloquence, Susan went to the electronic board and recorded what she had learned from the session:

Don't confuse participation with empowerment.

Two Nevers:

> *Never empower without goals.*
>
> *Never empower without a measurement.*

"That's really helpful," Charles told her excitedly. "I also learned from Doug's exposition that it's very dangerous to empower without the two M's. So why don't you study the goals part while I work on measurements? Okay?"

Susan smiled and nodded her head in agreement.

"Then," Charles concluded, "we'll both take another look at empowerment."

After they finished their meeting, there was left behind them on the electronic board Susan's contribution and the summary of the three management styles—the two traditional styles and the new one: GEM.

Styles of Management

Traditional	New
ODS	*GEM*
1. Autocratic 2. Participative (ODS – A) (ODS – P)	3. Empowering
Organize Deputize Supervise	Set Goals Empower Measure

Chapter 4

That's Not Empowerment: How Managers—and Companies— Delude Themselves

The following day, Charles and Susan met again in Charles' office for a brief session.

"I found the session with Doug Royal very helpful," Susan told him.

"I'm glad," Charles responded. "I've heard him speak on the subject before, but I seem to understand it better this time."

"Since we don't have much time today, I think we should just focus on what Doug told us and try to apply it to our own situation," Susan suggested.

"What do you mean?" Charles asked.

"I admit I wasn't very clear," she apologized. "Let me give you an example. In our division, we're using many of the labels that are part of GEM management—like empowerment and mission—but I think we're using them incorrectly."

"I see what you mean," Charles said after a moment's thought. "You're looking for the places where we're inconsistent with the GEM model."

"Yes," Susan replied. "Don't you think that's a good idea? We were given the assignment by our boss to push empowerment ahead in our division, and I think we both thought we were already doing it. But now it's clear to me that we haven't been doing much of it at all. We just thought we were."

"I think I have an example," Charles offered. "We have a mission statement, but we've been confusing it with having goals for empowered teams. Our mission statement is like the objective of a nation at war—we want to win the war. But that's too broad to be of much guidance to a middle-level officer in the field. So we think we have been providing goals, but we haven't. We've been deluding ourselves."

"Here's another example," said Susan. "We've been discussing a vision for our division. The current proposal is, 'to have the highest return to shareholders in our industry.' It's a nice sentiment, and some of the financial people are really turned on by it, but most of us aren't. I think it's simply too much of a pious hope—and it's very abstract. It certainly isn't the kind of vision that excited everyone at NASA. Remember Doug mentioned that vision—to put a person on the moon?"

"I remember," Charles said, "and I think you're right."

Susan added, "We should be writing some of this down."

She started to get up from her chair, but Charles jumped up first. "You did the writing before," he said. "Let me do it this time."

He positioned himself at the flip chart and wrote:

Cautions

- *A mission statement is not a mission or an adequate set of goals.*

- *A vision is not simply a pious hope.*

"We ought to add another one from our last conversation," Susan suggested. "It's one we've continually been doing wrong."

"What?" asked Charles.

"We tell people they're empowered when all we mean is that they're going to get to participate a bit more."

Charles nodded his head in agreement and wrote:

- *Participation is not empowerment.*

"And I have one," he offered.

"Then let's hear it," Susan said, looking pleased.

"We do almost no measurement to determine the success or failure of a team's mission."

"If any of our teams have real missions," Susan commented.

"Good point," Charles said, and he added:

- *Supervisors' oversight is not measurement.*

There was a pause as both lapsed into thought.

Charles suddenly broke the silence. "I have another example—one that I think is very important."

"Okay," Susan said. "What is it?"

"We've set up all these cross-functional teams and told them they're empowered. But they really aren't. They can't take any action without management approval. All they're really authorized to do is to make recommendations. They're not really empowered at all.

"Furthermore, the people on those teams are only there to carry out additional assignments. They also have their regular jobs, in which they report to their bosses. Now, when they meet in the team, no one knows who's actually speaking—a team member or a team member's boss. I mean, the team member may simply be parroting what the boss told him or her to say. So the discussion in the team doesn't necessarily reflect what its members genuinely think. The team's not really a team, and it's not empowered."

"You're right," Susan said excitedly, as if suddenly discovering a major truth. "We've got groups instead of teams, and they're advisory, not empowered. We've been creating committees—not empowered teams."

She urged Charles to put that observation on the flip chart, dictating as he wrote:

- *A committee isn't an empowered team.*

"Something you said brought an old experience to mind," Susan said. "I once attended the annual management conference of an international company. The chief executive officer was in his second year on the job. He'd made the management theme of his first year that the customer was to come first. At this second conference he wanted to make sure that his subordinates had gotten the message.

"'Suppose you come back to your office one day,' he said to the group, 'and find three messages. One is from the manager of our largest manufacturing plant: "We've a major problem," it says. "Call me immediately." Another is from your boss: "Call me immediately," it says. The third is from our largest customer: "Call me immediately," it says. Which message would you return first?' He repeated their options, and a vast majority of the hands went up when he said, 'The customer.'

"Then the CEO had each person take out a piece of paper and write down which call he or she would return first—that is, cast a secret ballot. The ballots were collected and counted. This time the result was . . ."

Charles smiled knowingly.

"You're right," Susan said. "The boss, by nine to one. Why? Because the boss makes or breaks a person's career. Wherever there is a boss-subordinate relationship, the boss will take first place with the subordinate. The customer will come second. And so will empowerment, because the subordinate will tend to wait for directions from the boss."

"Should I put that up?" Charles asked hesitantly. "I think we may be going a little too far."

"Put it up," said Susan. "If you disagree, put a question mark beside it."

Charles wrote on the flip chart with some evident reservation:

- *You can't have a traditional boss and be empowered.*

"Why didn't you add a question mark?" Susan asked.

"Because another example occurred to me," Charles said thoughtfully, "and it convinced me you're right about this. Remember three years ago when business was so bad in the transport division and people were starting to bail out? The top brass of our company decided they had to do something to stem the outflow of good people, so they held a three-day off-site meeting and invited all the most talented young people. I guess they figured

44

the older ones would probably stay, either out of loyalty or because they lacked other opportunities.

"Anyway, there were about one hundred people invited. For two days the brass explained the company's situation: its difficulties, its opportunities, its prospects. On the morning of the third day, they held a big question-and-answer session.

"As the morning drew to a close, one participant, an intense young man who'd sat for all three days in the front row, raised his hand to ask the chairman a question. When he was recognized, he gave his opinion of the situation.

"'I've been very impressed,' he said, 'by what I've heard here from our top management team in these several days. I think the team has a good plan for our company, and I'm much more optimistic than I was when I arrived. But you and others have continually referred to the lack of business. You've said that's one of the reasons why our firm is declining.

"Well, from my point of view, I don't see the situation at the plant in that way. Again and again, potential customers come to me with orders that depend on whether we can customize our service and products. I tell them that I'll check it out; then I ask my boss about it, and he passes the request up the chain of command while I wait, and wait. Finally, weeks later, I usually get approval, but when I call back the customer and say, 'Great news! We can do it for you,' the customer replies, 'That's nice, but your competitor agreed to do it for us a week ago. Sorry.' So, from my standpoint, our problem isn't a lack of business—it's that we're too bureaucratic to get the business.'

"This incident supports your point," Charles said, concluding his example. "I can see how having a hierarchy of bosses keeps employees from taking action. It does inhibit empowerment. I guess I agree with you about this after all."

"No need for the question mark then?" Susan asked.

Charles shook his head. "No need."

"Well, it seems we've accomplished something," she said, rising to her feet, "even though this has been a short meeting. I'm sorry I have to go now, but my other meeting is in fifteen minutes."

"That's all right," Charles replied, "I'd expected it. But before you leave we should decide what to do next. I think we ought to start considering how to implement GEM."

"I agree," Susan responded. "Any ideas?"

"Doug once suggested to me that there are five techniques for getting the new style underway. We could start there next time."

Susan said that was fine, and then she was gone. Behind her remained the list she and Charles had prepared to clarify the way companies and managers misunderstand what is essential for the transformation to the new management style.

Cautions

- *A mission statement is not a mission or an adequate set of goals.*
- *A vision is not simply a pious hope.*
- *Participation is not empowerment.*
- *Supervisors' oversight is not measurement.*
- *A committee isn't an empowered team.*
- *You can't have a traditional boss and be empowered.*

Chapter 5

The First Step—
Fault Tolerance

When Susan and Charles met again, he had just returned from Houston.

"So you finally got to Houston?" she asked.

"Yes."

"And did you see the fellow you wanted to? What was his name?"

"Philip Kowalski," Charles told her.

"Yes, Kowalski. Did you see him?"

"Yes."

"Well, how did it go? Why are you being so reticent?"

"Frankly, Susan," Charles said with exasperation, "I don't know how it went. Kowalski was very closely guarded. He listened, but he didn't tell me anything. I don't even know who's making the decision—Kowalski or Ron Jackson in Milwaukee. But when I mentioned Jackson, Kowalski got very suspicious, so I figured I was right in thinking I had to deal with one or the other, not both of them."

"Did you tell him about our interest in the division?"

"Yes. I spelled it all out. If they want to sell, we've got a good chance at getting the division."

"So you did well," Susan concluded triumphantly.

"I'm not at all sure," Charles replied flatly. "There's a good chance I went to the wrong place and the wrong person. I'm quite worried about it."

"About your career, you mean?" Susan asked.

"Yes, of course. At the end of the week our boss will be back. If I haven't had any good news from Houston by then—or if the news is bad—what will he say when he hears about all this? What if I went to the wrong place? He'll say, 'I sent you to Milwaukee, but you went to Houston and screwed up the deal. Are you crazy?'"

"Charles, you're being foolish!"

"I don't think so," he replied.

"Then this is a perfect application of the matter we were talking about last week, when we determined the conditions for empowerment. Remember, one condition was fault tolerance; without it, people won't make decisions and take risks."

"I remember," said Charles. "That was one of the techniques Doug Royal identified as essential for getting GEM underway. I didn't realize how quickly it would apply to me."

"Well, perhaps we should ask ourselves if it does apply." Susan suggested. "Let's suppose that you went to the wrong person and messed up the deal. Now, is that okay or not? I mean, in some circumstances it ought to be okay; otherwise, any mistake is a career disaster and no one will take any chances. Right?"

"Yes," Charles agreed grudgingly.

"Why are you so negative about this?" Susan asked.

"I guess I'm just suspicious about this line of reasoning," he explained rather plaintively, "because a company isn't in business to have people make mistakes, even me."

"Yes, that's true," Susan conceded, "but we agreed that there must be some fault tolerance if there's to be empowerment."

Charles snarled, "The closest we come to fault tolerance in this organization is that when someone makes a mistake, we ask: 'Do we hang him privately or publicly?'"

"That's absurd!" Susan burst out; but then she had to admit it was true. "And the fact that it is true means that it can't continue. Such an attitude is simply inconsistent with the transformation we're talking about in the company. So we have to use you as a case in point and ask ourselves, Is what Charles did a mistake? And if it is, should we tolerate it so that it doesn't affect his career—or not tolerate it?"

"Well, how do we do that?" Charles asked her.

"Let's suppose I'm the boss," suggested Susan. "Now, you come to my office to tell me why you shouldn't be blamed for screwing up the deal. What do you say?"

"Are you serious?"

"Yes, of course. This is important stuff," Susan insisted. "If we can't convince people that a mistake is okay sometimes, they won't take any action at all. I can recall a story I once heard. A middle-level manager made an error that cost the company millions. He was called to the chairman's office. 'Young man,' the chairman asked, 'do you know why I asked you to come here?' The young man replied, 'Yes, sir, you're going to fire me.' 'Fire you? Hell no!' said the chairman. 'I just spent ten million dollars educating you.'"

Charles laughed.

Susan continued: "But the line's not easy to draw, and many managers fail to get it right. We punish people for things we ought to overlook, and we accept things we ought to penalize; consequently, employees conclude the whole system is political—that right and wrong depends on who you know, not what you do—and they develop a pervasive mistrust. No one takes any action he or she isn't forced to take."

"All right," Charles agreed, "this is important stuff. Now where were we? I'm supposed to tell my boss why I ought to be excused from this error, right?"

"Right."

"Well, to begin with I'd say, 'This is the first time I've made a mistake like this. I've got a good record up to now. It ought to matter that this mistake is not part of a pattern, that it's unusual.'"

While Charles was speaking, Susan went over to the flip chart and put up the following heading:

When a Mistake Is Okay

Then she wrote under it:

- **When not part of a pattern**

She turned to Charles and commented, "You're right. Mistakes shouldn't be part of a pattern. The last thing our company needs is the problem of people who make mistake after mistake, but never the same one twice."

Charles grinned. He thought a moment and said, "And I'd say that we learned something from my mistake. We learned that it really is Ron Jackson who's in charge of the deal for Appex—although the boss will say he already knew that before I went off to Houston and screwed it all up."

Susan wrote:

- **When we learn something from it**

"I have one," Susan offered. "A mistake is okay when it's in pursuit of the goals or the mission." She wrote:

- **When it's in pursuit of the goals**

"But what else could it be in pursuit of?" Charles asked.

"Oh Charles, you're so straight," Susan chided. "It could be in pursuit of a private agenda. For example, you could have gone to Houston to see a girlfriend. And don't make a face, Charles. Even you could have a girlfriend."

Charles looked at her in surprise.

Susan laughed. "Gotcha," she said.

"How about an example of something less personal?" Charles asked.

"You could have been looking after the growth of your department, not the success of the business. If you had make a mistake while you were pursuing some private agenda—which happens all the time in a business—rather than while you were pursuing your mission for the company, then I don't see why the company should forgive it."

Charles shrugged in agreement.

"I'd say one other thing to my boss," he said, returning to their exercise.

"What?"

I'd say that it was within my authority to go to Houston, even if it was the wrong thing to do. It isn't as if I'd bet the company and lost."

"That's a good one, Charles."

Susan wrote on the chart:

- ### When it's within the scope of authority

"There's something else that should be added," Charles told her.

"What is it?"

"That whatever the person does should be consistent with the law and the basic values of the firm. In other words, if a person makes a mistake by violating the law or operating unethically, then it shouldn't be okay."

"You're absolutely right," Susan agreed, and added to her list:

- ### When it's consistent with law and company principles

Susan stepped back and admired her notes. "So now we have five criteria for when a mistake is okay. That's very good. Anything else to add?"

"I suppose," Charles ventured, "that we should add, 'when the proper procedures have been followed.'"

Susan looked at him in surprise. "Why should we include that?" she asked.

"Well, we don't want someone just jumping into decisions without proper preparation—shooting from the hip, so to speak— do we?"

"I'm not sure," she responded.

"Why not?" Charles asked.

"Well, because we already know the decision was a mistake. It's going to be difficult to decide whether the proper procedures were used, since we already know the outcome was bad. Somewhere a mistake was made in the procedures—something wasn't researched well enough, some base wasn't touched in advance, some calculation was in error, some event wasn't foreseen— otherwise, it would have worked out. I think it's only a form of scapegoating, which we do all the time now anyway. I guess I don't believe we'll find that proper procedures were used when we know the outcome was bad."

Charles shrugged. "I don't know," he said noncommittally.

"And there's something else," Susan said. "If I knew that I would be forgiven for making a mistake as long as I had followed proper procedures, then I'd be sure to dot every *i* and cross every

51

t before I took any action. That would slow everything up and drag supervisors into every little decision their employees make. It would be 'cover your behind' to the nth degree. I think it would only open the back door to all the bureaucratic behavior we're trying to throw out the front door."

Again Charles shrugged, as if not convinced.

"One last thing about this," Susan persisted. "If we have good, well-trained people whom we trust, why should we look over their shoulders? We know people have different styles of decision making. Some people study a problem to death before they act; they're very analytical, very methodical. Others are instinctive; they act on gut feelings. The more experienced they are, the more they may act without careful study. They recognize the situation and know—or think they know—just what to do. And often the intuitive types are our most successful people, right?"

Charles begrudgingly agreed.

"So if we look into process, we'll end up penalizing the intuitive and rewarding the methodical," Susan concluded. "Do we want to do that?"

"I still am uncomfortable with letting people get away with acting without an adequate process," Charles maintained stubbornly.

"All right," Susan conceded, "I'll put it up—but with a question mark to indicate that we don't totally agree on this."

She wrote:

- **When proper procedures were used (?)**

"Good," Charles said.

"I think we did very good work today," Susan said. "I appreciate your letting us use your situation as a guinea pig, Charles. I think this is a very important matter. Only if we can be specific about when a mistake is okay will we be able to induce people to actually make decisions, take actions, and accept risks. I think this is the key element of the cultural change we will need for empowerment."

She returned to the chart and wrote:

To convince people to act empowered, we must have an understanding of when mistakes are okay.

They both studied the list on the flip chart.

When a Mistake Is Okay

- **When not part of a pattern**

- **When we learn something from it**

- **When it's in pursuit of the goals**

- **When it's within the scope of authority**

- **When it's consistent with law and company principles**

- **When proper procedures were used (?)**

To convince people to act empowered, we must have an understanding of when mistakes are okay.

A few days later, in the course of reading a history book, Charles came upon a particularly interesting section. It drew examples from history to illustrate that for centuries people have been dealing with the question of when to hold a person responsible for an error in judgment. One of the most famous incidents took place in Britain, in the mid-1700s, when Admiral William Byng was condemned and executed for failing to engage a French fleet in the Mediterranean. Thomas B. Macaulay, the great nineteenth-century British historian, wrote the following critical commentary on the action that was taken:

> Byng was not found guilty of treachery, of cowardice, or of gross ignorance of his profession. He died for doing what the most loyal subject, the most intrepid warrior, the most experienced seaman, might have done. He died for

an error in judgment, an error such as the greatest commanders, Frederick, Napoleon, Wellington, have often committed and have often acknowledged. Such errors are not proper objects of punishment, for . . . the punishing of such errors tends not to prevent them, but to produce them. The dread of an ignominious death . . . has no tendency to bring out those qualities which enable men to form prompt and judicious decisions in great emergencies. . . . We cannot conceive of any thing more likely to deprive an officer of his self-possession at the time when he most needs it than the knowledge that, if the judgment of his superiors should not agree with his, he will be executed with every circumstance of shame. Queens, it has often been said, run far greater risks in childbed than private women, merely because their medical attendants are more anxious. The surgeon who attended Marie Louise [Napoleon's second empress] was altogether unnerved by his emotions. "Compose yourself," said Bonaparte; "imagine that you are assisting a poor girl in the Faubourg St. Antoine." This was surely a far wiser course than that of the Eastern king in the Arabian Nights' Entertainments, who proclaimed that the physicians who failed to cure his daughter should have their heads chopped off. Bonaparte knew mankind well; and, as he acted toward this surgeon, he acted towards his officers. No sovereign was ever so indulgent to mere errors of judgment; and it is certain that no sovereign ever had in his service so many men fit for the highest commands. (Thomas B. Macaulay, "William Pitt, Earl of Chatham," in *Macaulay's Historical Essays,* Thomas Nelson and Sons, London, 1924, pp. 205–206. The essay on Pitt was first published in 1834.)

Chapter 6

The Second Step—
Building Trust

One week passed before Susan and Charles were able to meet again. When they did, Susan was anxious to tell him about something that had happened to her during the week.

"I was asked to give a presentation to a group of sales managers from our company," she told Charles. "When I entered the room, I found them as angry as hornets. I asked what the problem was, and they told me that the supervisors of their units had just issued a directive to cut ten percent out of the travel and lodging item of each unit's budget.

"These are good people," Susan emphasized. "They weren't upset about the cost-cutting—everyone knows that the economy is in a recession and that the company has to draw in its belt. What infuriated them was that they were given no discretion in how and where to make the cost reductions. Some complained of needs for travel that now couldn't be met. Others spoke of items in their budgets that were too fat and could much more easily have been reduced.

"What rankled most of all was expressed in a comment made by several of the sales managers: 'They don't trust me.' That is to say, the top executives of their company didn't trust the managers to make intelligent decisions about their own units. 'We're being micro-managed,' I was told. 'The company tells us not only what to do, but how to do it.'

"I was struck by the reference to trust. When people say that others don't trust them, they usually are very bitter. A person who feels distrusted also feels unwanted or unappreciated. How will the company retain the services of people who feel like that?"

Susan paused to let Charles digest what she'd said.

After a few moments, he tried to summarize what he'd taken from her story.

"In effect," Charles said, "The people you talked to were saying, 'The company's top executives don't trust us, so they are micro-managing the business.' Is that right?"

"Exactly," Susan said. "When I talked with them I thought of our conversations about empowerment. These people wanted to be empowered. The company had told them that they were empowered, and they had believed it. Now the company micro-managed them, and they decided they weren't trusted. So empowerment has become an issue of trust."

"What a change in attitude!" Charles exclaimed. "Years ago, when I joined this company, our CEO used to say, 'Managers must manage.' I remember his words very well. What he meant was that managers were supposed to direct closely what their subordinates did. But, as you said, today more and more subordinates view close direction not as a legitimate function of management, but as an unnecessary interference in their activities that is motivated by mistrust."

"That's it," Susan agreed. "The people I talked with were saying, 'We're responsible for the profitability of our branches, but we aren't given control of our budgets. It isn't right that we should be held accountable when we don't have the power to achieve the results.'"

"This is a big thing," Charles said. "What we have here is a change in how key employees think about the company. It's an emerging expectation, and such a thing is an extremely powerful force in business; however, because it occurs only on a broad time scale, it's significance is often missed.

"Once I studied the background of participative management, what Doug Royal would call the ODS-participative system of management. It began about forty years ago when professionals in Northern Europe and North American began to insist that they had a right to participate in business decisions that would affect them. Slowly the conviction grew that unless a person was consulted by his or her boss about a key decision before it was made, the person had no moral obligation to carry out the decision except in a pro-forma way. Today, almost everyone feels that way.

"This expectation, which started in a small way three decades ago and snowballed over the years, is the cause of the participation revolution in the traditional management style. As a result, most managers today invite their subordinates to participate to some degree in decision making.

"It may be," he concluded, "that today we are in the early stages of another revolution of equal significance. Again, it originates with professionals who have skills that are in demand and who feel free to move in search of what they want in the workplace—like the sales managers with whom you were talking. This time the expectation has moved beyond participation to empowerment—to independence and autonomy in how people go about pursuing their goals. If they don't receive independence, they don't feel obliged to give full commitment to the firm or to fully buy into the goals it has set. Companies are likely to be forced to respond to this new expectation, just as they've been forced to respond over the past several decades to the demand for participation."

"We ought to talk about trust," Susan said, "because I think it's really important in the new style of management. Now that we've delayered and downsized our organization, there's a new dimension of importance to people trusting each other.

"We're going to have work conducted by teams, and there won't be enough supervisors for them to closely oversee workers. Also, the scoring system for how well an individual is doing in his or her job may be less clear."

"And," interjected Charles, "it's uncertain who the score-keeper is."

Susan smiled in agreement. "I think," she said, "that a modern organization which is characterized by participation, empowerment, teamwork, shared values, and leadership requires high levels of trust among managers and employees to be able to function efficiently. Trust is what makes it possible for people to work together when they are concerned about themselves yet need to cooperate to make the business successful.

"It's essential that people feel free to tell the truth, because the truth is the key to effective decision making. If we managers lack the whole truth, we can't fix problems or plan sensible strategies. Consequently, if people won't trust our company, they themselves won't tell the truth; instead, they'll pass forward only good news and go to great extremes to cover their mistakes."

"It's worse than that," Charles said grimly as Susan paused. "I think that people won't just withhold bad information but also distort what they communicate. Without trust, the openness we are seeking with GEM management may become a swamp of lies and misinformation."

Susan nodded her head. "So what is crucial to us," she said, "is truth, and trust makes truth possible. In this sense, trust is the glue that holds the organization together."

"It's peculiar," Charles mused. "It seems that writers and consultants have put considerable energy into describing the new organizations: their openness, the crossing of boundaries, teamwork, information sharing. But what's it like inside the most effective of these organizations? That's what you and I are talking about. How do the dynamics of managerial behavior change? When a manager can't oversee closely, how does he or she build the trust necessary for getting things done right? How is the new glue—not overseeing, but trust—applied?"

"Well," Susan responded, "there's a naive notion that trust means everyone agrees—that we're all one big happy family, so to speak. In my opinion, the idea that trust automatically results in peace and harmony is very much mistaken; instead, what is important is that trust permits people to state their minds openly and to disagree with one another. It even permits some to make mistakes. It creates an environment likely to be filled with contention as people support their own points of view."

"But even though there's disagreement, people can disagree politely," Charles added.

"Yes," Susan said. "In fact, the more serious the disagreements and the more open the communication between people, the more important it is to be polite, because otherwise people get angry at one another and trust breaks down."

"So what we're saying," Charles suggested, "is we don't want an organization that is harmonious just because those in it are afraid to tell the truth or to advance different perspectives. Right?"

"Right," Susan replied, adding, "Because it won't be effective."

"I've been working on trust myself this past week," Charles told her. "It's interesting that we both came to the conclusion that this is a key area in the transition to GEM management."

"What influenced your thinking?" Susan asked.

"I had another talk with Doug Royal," Charles answered. "I wanted to include you, but you were busy elsewhere. I thought about holding off my discussion with him until you could join us, but I wasn't sure we could get him here again soon."

"It was fine for you to go ahead," Susan answered him. "What did you talk about with Doug?"

"We had a very interesting discussion on trust. I'd always thought about trust as one thing—you either trust someone or you don't. But Doug made me think about different aspects of trust. He said that there were three key levels of trust."

"Levels of trust?" Susan asked, her eyes narrowing suspiciously. "How would there be levels of trust? I agree with you—you either trust someone or you don't."

"Doug said that wasn't so," Charles replied. "He said that in business there are three levels of trust. Each is important, but the more levels achieved, the greater the capability of the firm to act effectively."

Following their previous practice, he went to the flip chart and wrote on it:

Three Levels of Trust
Level One: Predictability

"This is the lowest form of trust," Charles explained, "but even it provides some degree of comfort to people in the workplace. It simply means that the company (or an individual manager, for that matter) acts in a way that is consistent with its own interests. The employee may not share those interests, and even may be exploited in the process, but at least he or she can anticipate what is likely to happen.

"For example, an employee might say, 'No matter what my company says it will do, it always takes the cheapest way out.' Then the employee might add, 'I can trust them to do that.' It's not a very high level of trust, but it's better than complete unpredictability."

"I can think of an example," Susan put in. "I remember my friend Carol, years ago, talking about a supervisor who gave her a lot of trouble because of her race. She said, 'My manager is a real bigot, but at least I know where he stands. I don't like the way I'm treated, but I can always predict what he's going to do. In some ways that's better than having him mouth fine sentiments only to discriminate against me when I'm not expecting it—like other people sometimes do.'"

"That's a good example," Charles agreed. "Now let's go to level two."

On the chart he wrote:

Level Two: Reliability

"The question here," Charles began to explain, "is fairly simple: When a manager or a company promises something to employees, can the employees rely on its being carried through? If the answer is yes, then the company can be trusted to carry through on its promises. It's reliable—and that's better than merely predictable.

"When Doug was talking about this level of trust, I remembered something that one of your former workers told me about you." He paused and grinned at his colleague.

Susan looked at him quizzically. What's coming? she wondered.

"I can remember being told that 'Susan's not a bad boss. When she says she's going to do something, I can trust her to do it. If I ask for something and she says okay, even though she may not want to and even though it may cost the company something, she'll carry through on it. She won't break her commitment by

60

using an excuse such as 'I didn't know how much it would cost,' or 'My boss told me I couldn't do it.'"

"That's not so bad," she said, relieved.

"I thought it was pretty good," Charles responded.

"Another example," Susan said, "would be an employee saying: 'I know the rules and the company knows them. I stick to them, and they're consistent in sticking to the rules. I can rely on them for that.'"

She barely finished speaking before Charles began to write on the chart:

Level Three: Mutuality

When Susan read the word *mutuality,* a puzzled look came over her face. "What's that?" she asked.

"According to Doug, mutuality is the highest level of trust," Charles explained. "It means that employees believe their managers and/or companies know what matters to employees and have adopted, or internalized, their employees' goals.

"An employee might say, 'I trust the company because it cares about me. It knows what matters to me. It has made my goals its own.' Mutuality is based on caring.

"It's also a two-way street: the employee trusts the firm, and the firm trusts the employee. The employee should be predictable, reliable, and caring, as well as the firm. The firm cares about the employee's welfare, and the employee cares about the firm's success in the business.

"When the employee trusts the firm completely, he or she does two things that we absolutely need employees to do in the difficult business situation we're in. First, they will share with the firm their knowledge of how to improve our productivity and efficiency. They hold back if they're afraid for their jobs, hoping to make themselves needed. Second, a trusting employee will be much more adaptable, much more ready to accept change and make it work. In a business environment dominated by competition and change, these two factors are crucial. But if people don't think we in management care about them, they won't help us."

Charles paused a moment, then provided an example: "Once I attended a meeting between one of our top executives and a group of young people who worked for the firm. They had an open and increasingly candid interchange. Finally one of the younger people commented, 'I don't think the company really cares about me as a person.' The executive was shocked. 'What do you mean we don't care about you?' he demanded. 'We pay the best salaries in our industry and we provide the best benefits. You have the best opportunities for promotion.'

"The young man listened to the executive with a look of total amazement on his face. When the executive was finished, he responded softly, 'It would never occur to me to think of those things as evidence of caring.' He went on to explain that caring meant the executive should understand what matters to the employee as an individual and try to assist the employee in achieving it. Among the things that mattered to him, he added, were his family, his personal development, and the security of his employment. It wasn't that salary and benefits weren't important, he explained, but that they were contractual in nature, entitlements that depended on whether he did his job well, and not reflective of a deeper relationship between himself and the company."

"Wow!" Susan exclaimed. "We don't do very well at that, do we?"

"What do you mean?" Charles asked.

"Well, because managers and executives are told today that they owe their primary allegiance to shareholders, and because shareholders generally think of a company as an instrumentality—one that is intended to increase their wealth—we often forget that to many employees a company is more than a mere instrumentality. It is a sort of second family. And in the past, people could count on having a lifetime job if they performed reasonably well—and sometimes even if they didn't.

"I think that before the 1980s many large firms like ours provided substantial employment security to many of their employees. A manager was expected to have a position for his or her entire career; many clerical employees had similar expectations because their firms were growing and prospering financially; blue-collar workers with seniority were protected by union contracts from layoff except in the most severe business downturns;

and we provided employment security for white-collar employees because we didn't lay them off. But now all this has changed.
We've done so much downsizing, getting rid of jobs of all ranks.

"The attitude of top management has changed too. I remember
our CEO telling us last year when we were discussing motivation
in our company: 'We don't expect to provide secure jobs. We'll
replace anyone whenever it will help us to increase profits, and
we have to expect that anyone we employ will jump to another
firm if it will improve his or her financial situation. We don't
expect any loyalty from our employees, and we don't give them
any. As managers, we have to learn to manage without loyalty.'

"I was so shocked, but as I thought about it, I decided that I
admired our CEO for saying clearly what everyone had come to
recognize but wouldn't talk about. In effect, our company has
little or no long-term commitment to its employees, and expects
no substantial commitment from them."

"What Doug Royal would say," Charles added, "is that without some degree of reciprocated security and loyalty, extended
from company to employee and from employee to company,
mutual trust—which is based on reciprocal commitment—cannot
exist."

"How can employees give a company security?" Susan asked.

"What?"

"You said there should be 'reciprocated security and loyalty,
extended from company to employee and from employee to
company.' How can an employee give a company security?"

"Oh, I didn't understand your question at first," Charles said.
"An employee can't give a company security, but a group of
employees can. I was using 'employee' in a collective sense. They
give a company security by being fully committed to it and
willing to do what is necessary to make it a success. Most people
don't do that—as you well know. They take direction from their
supervisors, do what they're told to do, and don't pay much
attention to whether the result helps the company or not."

"Like the unpleasant attitude we sometimes encounter from
bank tellers, or personnel at airline-ticket counters, or retail
salespeople," Susan added.

"Yes," Charles replied. He paused, then stated rhetorically: "Why don't American companies pursue the highest level of trust? Because they believe it will be too expensive financially, and because the American investor community doesn't recognize how valuable it is for a company to have the full trust of its employees. That's why."

"In some ways, it's strange," Susan commented. "The purpose of business is supposed to be to create a profitable company. To achieve that, the commitment of employees is key. I think employee effort is a lot more important to the success of the business than that of the shareholders. All the shareholders put up is money. In addition, many of them, if not most of them, have no long-term commitment to the firm—they come and go, seeking the highest return they can find. But employees are here day after day, making an effort, and most want to stay. They have a different and deeper involvement in the firm than the shareholders. They have the potential to make a much greater contribution to the success of the firm than the shareholders. And the shareholders want the business to be successful because it will give them a good return on their investment. So you'd think that the shareholder would want the company to do whatever it could to build trust and commitment in the employees, instead of pushing the company to create insecurity and demolish loyalty. If you were a shareholder, wouldn't you feel that way?"

"Yes," Charles said. "It seems counterproductive for shareholders to press insecurity on employees; however, from their point of view it appears productive."

"Why do you think that is?" Susan asked.

"It must be because they believe two things: that insecure, frightened employees work harder and better than those who are secure, and that many of the dollars which go to employees in a business downturn ought to go to the shareholders instead."

"But that's very short-term thinking," Susan objected. "It means that the shareholders get a few more dollars now instead of many more later."

"So shareholders have a focus on the present," Charles responded, grinning. "What else is new? Most of them are traders, not investors, and are looking for the quick gain."

"So we can't build mutuality in the company because we can't recognize that the employees have a special relationship with the success of the firm?"

"Oh, we can recognize it," Charles answered. "We just can't act on it—can't do anything about it."

"It's very frustrating to see something that would help us run the company better," Susan said, "and yet not be able to do it. We can't approach Doug's third level of trust because we have to leave the employees thinking: I don't really trust the company because it doesn't care about me."

"As we've been discussing this," Charles said, "it's occurred to me that a manager can build the first two levels of trust on his or her own; the third level can only be built by the manager with the cooperation of the firm. This is because a manager cannot individually provide employment security for his or her people. If the firm says to downsize, we have to let people go."

"But that doesn't stop some managers from suggesting to employees that they have security," Susan told him. "The manager suggests that somehow he or she can protect the employees' jobs; then, when those managers are forced to make layoffs, they lose the trust of employees completely."

"I've made that mistake myself," Charles acknowledged wryly.

"Okay," Susan said. "Doug has helped us understand trust, even though he's not here and you did it for him."

Charles smiled at her compliment.

"So now we have to ask, How do we build trust in our firm?" Charles wrote on the flip chart:

Building Trust: The Key Steps

"The first level of trust was predictability, wasn't it?" Susan asked.

"Yes," Charles answered, writing:

Building Predictability

"Now how do we do that?" he asked.

"I have an idea," Susan said. "I think in the context of the workplace, trust is a personal conviction that depends on people getting to know their co-workers, especially outside the work environment. People trust you when they know you well enough to be able to predict what you'll do in a situation."

"That's not a very high level of trust," Charles objected.

"No, it isn't," she agreed. "But we're talking about the lowest level of trust, aren't we?"

"Yes, you're right. I guess I was just thinking that we can build a higher order of trust when we get close to people personally."

"Yes, we can," Susan concurred. "But don't forget that with all the delayering, we managers have so many people we're responsible for that we can't get to know them as well as we could in the past."

Charles nodded in agreement. "It's funny. Even before we delayered—when we had only a few people reporting to us—many of us who are managers still didn't want to get to know the people well. I think we thought we were trying to preserve our objectivity by not getting too close to people. Consequently, many personal relationships were shallow and didn't promote trust."

He wrote:

- *Make personal contact.*

Charles left the chart and returned to his chair.

"You know," he said, "I once worked with an executive whose actions contradicted almost every pronouncement he made. The result was that everyone in his management team distrusted him so profoundly that the entire organization virtually ceased to function. He did everything wrong a person could do."

Susan listened closely as he recounted the executive's errors, which included:

- sending conflicting signals
- explaining many of his actions with a lie or half-truth
- overruling decisions of his management team without explanation
- encouraging subordinates to take actions, then reversing them

- insisting on managing processes of which he was igno-
  rant
- telling everyone there would be no discharges, then fir-
  ing two people and threatening to fire all the others
- changing the old rules, but announcing no new ones
- insisting he be accepted as one of the group of his subordinates, then pulling rank to get his own way
- after all the above, insisting that no one understood him
  and that he was unjustly criticized

"Amazing," Susan said. "I think inconsistency will always be
perceived by people as lack of dependability at best and as
hypocrisy at worst. Either way, it undermines trust."

She went to the chart and added to Charles' list:

- *Be consistent.*

Then she continued: "I think a manager's success creates in
his associates a certain level of confidence in him, and does so
even if there is little personal contact among the people involved—at a distance, so to speak. So I'll add it to our list."

- *Be successful.*

"I think that's enough about predictability," Charles suggested. "Let's go on to reliability."

Susan wrote:

Building Reliability

"According to Doug, reliability is the second level of trust,"
Charles explained. "It means that a person can trust his or her
superior or the company to do whatever has been promised, even
if it is inconvenient or costs the firm money. It means a person
can rely on the company or a superior to keep a commitment."

"I can understand that," Susan responded. "I think nothing so
undermines people's trust as the conviction that someone has let
them down or betrayed them." She paused. "But I think that often
what is perceived as betrayal is usually a result of misunderstand-
ing—and usually built around unwarranted expectations. For
example, employees who are expecting a promotion can be
infuriated when it doesn't materialize or when their supervisors

don't include them in the selection process. When this happens, the aggrieved person will almost always view the outcome as a betrayal and will cease to trust the manager.

"Yet the manager may never have intended to support the person for a promotion. Why then the confusion? Perhaps the manager found it expedient to lead the employee on, letting him or her believe a promotion was in the offing in order to get a higher effort from the person. Or perhaps the employee thought his or her potential much higher than did the manager, but the manager was reluctant to create a conflict by being open about personal expectations.

"To get to the point," Susan smiled at her own long-windedness, "I think that to build reliability we have to keep promises."

She turned to the flip chart and wrote:

- *Keep promises.*

"But," she continued, "I also think we have to set the right level of expectations. In a crucial way, trust requires openness. It isn't that openness is trust; it's that openness creates an environment in which expectations are reasonable enough for managers to meet them. Then, when people see management living up to expectations and being reliable, they trust management.

"Conversely, if a manager can't encourage performance without misleading people, then he or she can't expect to build trust in the organization. In other words, if a manager can't be open with subordinates about their performance and potential, then he or she can't expect to be trusted."

"Therefore, it's crucial to be direct about where a person stands," said Charles, picking up Susan's theme. "We have to do that in performance evaluations and in the ordinary day-to-day interaction among managers and employees. When expectations are similar, disappointments are less likely and trust can be maintained."

"Right," said Susan emphatically, and she wrote:

- *Let people know where they stand.*

Suddenly Charles looked worried. "But don't the less well defined roles of the flattened organizations make it more difficult for managers to let people know where they stand?" he asked.

"No," Susan answered without hesitation. "Not at all. I thought about that last week. First, being open about performance doesn't require telling a person precisely what to do, as in ODS management; it doesn't involve giving detailed directions, but giving an honest evaluation of performance. If promotions are likely to be few and awarded only to the truly outstanding, and if everyone understands that, then correct aspirations have been set, even though it may not be possible to specify exactly what will win a promotion for a person. For example, salespeople often compete for prizes that go to the person who sells the most. How much a person must sell in order to win cannot be announced in advance. 'How much do I have to sell to win?' asks a salesperson. Responds the sales manager: 'However much is more than your competitors sell.' The lack of precision about the exact amount to be sold is not a problem."

Charles nodded, accepting her position; then he said, "I have another item for our list."

He walked over to the chart, took the marker Susan offered him, and wrote:

- *Support each other.*

"As we were talking about trust," he said "the strangest recollection came to me, of a quote I once read in a book on the Civil War. It's something William Tecumseh Sherman said about Ulysses S. Grant after they had worked together for many years, during the war and following it. I'm not sure if you know this, but Sherman had bouts of insanity and sometimes was confined for them. He even came close to losing his military career because of them, but Grant always supported him. And Grant had a severe problem with alcohol. When he was asked about their relationship, Sherman said, "'Grant and I trust each other completely. He stood by me when I was crazy, and I stood by him when he was drunk, and now we always stand by each other no matter what.'

"We said earlier that trust is largely built on personal contact that goes beyond mere friendliness. For people to really trust one another they have to have been through difficulties together—to

69

have supported one another in adversity. Trust is built when things go wrong just often as it is built when they go right. I can trust a person who brings me success, and I can trust a person who stands by me when I get in trouble."

Susan smiled, amused by the story about Sherman and Grant.

"The steps we've listed on the chart are sufficient to build trust at the first and second level," she pointed out, "but they're not sufficient to build it at the third level."

"I was thinking that too," Charles agreed. "If the company won't—or can't—provide employment security for people, the company can't expect people to fully trust their employer. And a single manager can't do what the firm won't do, so we can't really hope to build full mutuality. But I think there are several steps that can carry us at least part of the way.

"We can at least care about our people as individuals. Even in a delayered environment, where we don't have time to closely supervise people, we can still find time to care about them. It's often been pointed out that history's great military leaders—Alexander, Napoleon, and George Patton among them—could depend on the intense loyalty of their troops. This loyalty was based on the soldiers' conviction that their leader really cared about them and would try to ensure their safety."

Charles wrote on the chart:

Building Mutuality
- *Take time to care.*

"There's another thing we can do," Susan suggested. "When we downsize, we can make a concentrated effort to complete the process quickly, so that those who remain can have some confidence that they'll retain their jobs. Then we can offer at least a short-term expectation of employment security."

Charles nodded, and wrote:

- *Provide as much security as possible.*

Charles and Susan looked at their full chart and nodded with approval to each other.

Charles then commented, "I think we should also add some of the pitfalls."

"Pitfalls?" Susan asked.

"Yes, of trying to manage by trust."

"Are there some?"

"Absolutely," Charles insisted. He threw over the page on the flip chart and wrote at the top of a clean sheet:

Pitfalls in Managing by Trust

Charles explained: "Many consultants tell managers to build trust by having open communications, by meeting employees in informal setting, by encouraging a free exchange of views, and by involving people in decisions. All this is good in an environment characterized by trust; however, where there is little trust among the individuals involved, these things can backfire. Information freely available can be used in office politics to destroy a person, informal access can be used to spread rumor, and participation can be misused to seize personal credit where it isn't deserved."

He wrote on the chart:

- *Unreciprocated trust that can be used against you*

"I don't think most employees will take advantage of a manager who is really trustworthy," Susan said, "but it's not easy to manage by trust. Many managers who recognize the importance of trust in an organization, and who want to build their relationships on trust, find it difficult to do so. Many talk about trust, claiming they trust people, but then in practice try to keep close control; they're afraid that if they don't, they'll be fooled by subordinates. It's no surprise that employees respond to the actions of their managers and not the words. Then these managers complain that employees don't act as if they're trusted. Well, they don't act as if they're trusted precisely because they aren't really trusted."

"That executive you mentioned earlier was trying to use words to counteract his actions," Susan pointed out, "but I don't think you can simply talk your way out of a situation into which your actions have put you."

Charles wrote:

- *Not trusting enough*

"The situation is sometimes worse than a manager failing to act on his or her words," Charles said. "There's a pathological behavior I've seen in some of our company managers. I call it . . ." and he wrote:

- *False trust*

Charles explained: "I think that, in many respects, acting as if you trust someone when you don't is the worse thing a manager can do, and the most demoralizing to employees.

"I've seen numerous examples of managers who pervert the need for trust in their organizations by insisting that employees behave as if there were a climate of trust, then betraying it. In some instances, unscrupulous managers knowingly turn trust to their own advantage, and in doing so, undermine it for the firm. In others, well-meaning managers try to behave in the new fashion, but fall back into the old pattern of mistrust. Whatever the cause, the result is disastrous.

"For a number of years I've watched a manager in another division of our firm who has become a very vocal exponent of a new culture of trust and openness. He very eloquently espouses an ethic of trust, participation, and empowerment, but underneath it all, he's highly manipulative.

"'It's hypocrisy,' one of his subordinates said to me. 'Egos are running rampant here. Some people are playing the role of new-culture champions. But my manager hasn't really opened up at all; he's just substituted one set of rules for another. Either you play the game his way, or he'll find a way to get you out. Several people have had it up to here with the hypocrisy. At least one has quit, and another is about to.'

"Another one of his people told me: 'My manager's disappeared. He heard that in the new culture you can't be too directive, so he's disappeared.' Added yet another: 'You can't pin our manager down. He's like a ball of mercury—he just keeps scooting across the table.'

"I asked them how they cope with that manager who expresses the ethic of openness and honesty but refuses to tolerate dissent or differences of opinion. One told me: 'My manager is just like a teenager. He's bullheaded. I've discovered that the way to deal with him is to agree instantly to whatever he says; then, as soon as he walks out of the room, you resume doing whatever you think is best for the company.'

"The result of the false promise of trust is distrust. 'Ask any of the professionals,' I was told. 'We distrust this whole thing. That's it! If there's one word that sums up my feelings about my manager, it's *distrust*.'"

"You think this guy is intentionally manipulating his people, don't you?" Susan asked.

"Yes, I do," Charles responded, his voice still hot with indignation.

"You're probably right," Susan said. "But let's think about the possibility that he's trying to do the right thing but doesn't know how. What exactly is he doing wrong?"

"Well," replied Charles, willing to go along with Susan's premise. "First, he has a false conception of trust as a kind of gooey good feeling. He's assuming it means that everyone should agree. The old culture of mistrust was divisive and tension-filled, so he thinks the new culture of trust should be cohesive and peaceful—and to a degree it should be. But honesty means an opportunity to openly disagree. In a culture of trust, this does not necessarily destroy unity or create tension. In fact, real trust creates an environment in which disagreements and conflicts can be made explicit, be addressed, and be resolved. When people trust one another, they welcome differences of opinion; they're thankful for the truth, even when the news isn't good, because it allows them to take corrective measures over time. Our manager hasn't yet grasped this.

"Second, our manager has confused participation and delegation with abdication. He no longer makes decisions that should be his; he fails to provide leadership. In its place is the gooey good feeling he confuses with trust."

After pausing for a moment, Charles concluded, "There, I've answered your question—although I really think he's just a manipulative hypocrite who knows what he's doing."

Susan shrugged. She didn't agree, but seeing no purpose in arguing about the matter, she said, "An executive once told me about the best boss he ever had. 'Why was he so good?' I asked. The man responded, 'When things were going well, he would push me, try to keep me from getting complacent. And when things were bad, he'd ask what he could do to help.

"'Most executives,' he added, 'are just the opposite. When things are going well, they praise you; when things are going badly, they kick you. But it's when things are going well that you need the goad, and it's when they're going badly that you need the help. When your boss does that for you, then you know he trusts you, and you don't hesitate to tell him the truth.'

"I think the point is that we don't trust each other enough for us to share our thoughts about the business or the company, or even a vision of the future. We don't trust each other enough in this company to begin building the company we all want to have.

"I think the real question about trust is this: Are you willing to let me be myself? Or will I get slammed, fired, for being myself? Do we trust each other enough to let down the masks? This is a key issue for many people."

"I think you're right, Susan," Charles said. "I have two more recommendations for our list."

He wrote:

The Maxims of Trust

Always aim for the highest level of trust you can achieve.

Never presume you've been given more trust than you have earned.

Charles and Susan tore their two used sheets off the flip chart and taped them to the wall. They stood back and admired their handiwork.

Three Levels of Trust
Level One: Predictability
Level Two: Reliability
Level Three: Mutuality

Building Trust: The Key Steps

Building Predictability
- Make personal contact.
- Be consistent.
- Be successful.

Building Reliability
- Keep promises.
- Let people know where they stand.
- Support each other.

Building Mutuality
- Take time to care.
- Provide as much security as possible.

Pitfalls in Managing by Trust

- Unreciprocated trust that can be used against you
- Not trusting enough
- False trust

The Maxims of Trust

Always aim for the highest level of trust you can achieve.

Never presume you've been given more trust than you have earned.

Chapter 7

The Third Step—*Vision*

When Charles joined Susan in a deserted conference room for their next discussion session, he immediately noticed that Susan's attitude had changed. In place of her usual detached, almost academic demeanor and curiosity, he now found an intense, no-nonsense approach. Susan was all business today.

Gently he inquired about the change.

"I've been told to straighten out our Southwestern retail division," she told him curtly. "I've got to get to work."

"Do you have time to meet with me today?" Charles asked, ready to depart at her request.

"I've been thinking about it," she responded. They were well enough acquainted that she felt no need to soothe his ego by qualifying her comment with a statement like "I've enjoyed our discussions and would like to continue them, if only I had time."

Although he understood, Charles was nonetheless slightly offended at her sharpness. Expecting to be dismissed, he grasped the arms of his chair and slid to the edge of his seat; but then, Susan said something quite surprising.

"I've been taking GEM management seriously," she told him. "Now I've been given an assignment. I want to see if it fits our thinking. Have I been empowered or not? Is my boss using GEM here, or isn't he?"

Charles released his hold on the arms of his chair and allowed himself to sink back down into the cushion. He wasn't going anywhere, at least not for a while.

"Where should we begin?" he asked.

"I was trying to remember the distinctions Doug Royal gave us when we met with him," Susan said. "He talked about vision, and mission and goals . . ."

"I think I understood what he was saying," Charles offered. "Let's see if we can apply it here. Then we can go on to see if the goals you've been given make sense. Okay?

"Perfect," Susan replied.

"He started with vision. Do you have a vision for what you're doing?"

Susan objected. "I think you mean 'Is there a corporate vision that will help me direct my efforts?'"

Charles smiled. "That's what I meant," he acknowledged.

"You know about that as much as I do," she said.

Charles continued to grin. "Whenever I hear the word *vision* I think of something two of my friends explained to me a few days ago. One's a commercial airline pilot making a hefty salary and enjoying lots of time off for his other interests. It's a great job. And he has a buddy—I know them both—who's in the Air Force as a navigator on big cargo jets. He gets paid a whole lot less than the commercial pilots and has none of the perks.

"They've been friends for a long time. Even trained for Viet Nam together, and then stayed there for several years. Since the war, one has done very well as a pilot, while the other has been stuck in the military service. I asked them why their careers had taken such different turns.

"They told me that it all went back to flight school in the Air Force, before the war. One of them took pilot training; the other prepared to be a navigator. After the war the pilot had lots of opportunities to fly commercial jets, so he did very well. But the commercial carriers took the navigators off their planes—they were displaced by technology, I guess the airlines would say—so the other guy couldn't work outside the military.

"I asked the pilot, 'How did you know to become a pilot and not a navigator?'

"He answered me with one word: *Vision.*

"'Vision?' I nearly shouted. 'Vision? You mean that even then, in the late 1960s, you saw that after the war there'd be good-paying civilian jobs for pilots but not for navigators? You saw way back then that technology would develop to a point where it would displace navigators from commercial aircraft?'

"I was getting really excited. You and I and Doug had been talking about vision in our company, and here was a guy who clearly had demonstrated it. 'How did you do it?' I wanted to know. 'How did you develop that vision of the future?'

"He looked at me as if I were a total fool. 'No, no!' he said. 'Vision, vision! I passed the eyesight test required to be a pilot; my friend didn't.'"

Charles sat back and laughed. Despite her no-nonsense frame of mind, Susan joined in.

"You can see," Charles said, "how sophisticated and abstract my thinking had become. Someone said 'vision' and I immediately thought of management theory. He had to remind me that vision is first of all about eyesight." He kept laughing.

"All right," Susan said, serious once again, "let's get back to business—unless there's some point to your story other than that you made a mistake."

"There is a point, a small point," Charles replied. "A vision isn't the same thing as a prediction of the future; it doesn't enable people to forecast changes in technology. That's what I had assumed my friend meant by it. The way we and Doug are using it, it's something else."

"Well, that is helpful," Susan commented. "A vision is something we want to have, but not a blueprint. It can't be a blueprint because that requires too much specificity, right?"

"Right," Charles confirmed. "I thought about a vision after that discussion with my friend, and I decided that a vision is something that seems impossible for us in the immediate future. It's something we want to do or to be, but that looks like too much to achieve. That's its value—it causes us to stretch. Developing a good vision is a matter of real leadership, because people have to buy into it—believe in it—even though it seems unattainable. The leader has to help others see in themselves the potential and ability to achieve something that looks impossible."

"Do we have a vision in our company?" Susan asked.

"I don't think so. We have a purpose: to make money for our shareholders. We have financial targets to spell out that purpose.

79

But the purpose and the targets hardly constitute a vision. I mean, a vision ought to inspire us. Only an accountant—"

"Or our CEO," Susan interjected with a cynical sneer.

"—would be turned on by our financial targets," Charles finished.

"What would be a good vision?" Susan asked. "I mean, I can't do it for our company, but I might be able to for my new division."

"It might help you to have a concept of a vision for our firm, too," Charles suggested, "even if it's only one you and I created. Then you could plug your division's own vision into the overall corporate one."

"Good idea," Susan replied. "Do you know of any good visions?"

"I think we both have heard about several," Charles said. "Perhaps the best ever was NASA's vision to put a man on the moon. Think of it. It must have appeared almost impossible at the beginning, in the early 1960s, but it gripped the attention of scientists and technicians, and ultimately, the attention of the entire nation. People knew what the overall objective was and aligned themselves with the purpose."

"That was great," Susan acknowledged. "But a corporation can't be that specific."

"I think it can," Charles said. "For example, one form of corporate vision is to best a dominant competitor; for example, Komatsu had the vision 'Kill Caterpillar.'"

"They didn't do a very good job," Susan said.

"Well, Caterpillar may be killing itself," Charles replied.

"I don't like that kind of vision. It's too negative," she said. "'Kill your competitor.' I don't like it."

"I have in mind a different kind of corporate vision," Charles said. "It goes with a story that I think is one of the most poignant in business history. You know that Xerox had the personal computer developed in its California lab for years before Apple came along, but Xerox never got it to the marketplace. It's one of the great missed opportunities in business history."

"No, I didn't know that," Susan said.

"I heard about it from a business magazine reporter who interviewed me once," Charles explained. "He had just written a story about Xerox's chairman, who told him about the episode during an interview. Although the information was for the record, the magazine's editors had cut it out of the story they published.

"The Xerox executive told the reporter that he had known about his firm's failure to get the PC to market in the 1970s, and that when he became chairman, he looked into the matter to learn how to avoid such errors in the future. In brief, he said he was convinced Apple brought the PC to market first and his company never got it out because, at that time, Apple had a corporate vision and Xerox didn't. At Xerox the sole objective was to make money, and no one in Xerox could ever convince themselves there was enough demand for the PC to make it profitable for them to produce the PC for the marketplace.

"But Apple hardly even asked that question. Apple had a vision. It wanted to take the computer out of the glass house—the central facility where the mainframe sat and that no one could access except the information technology people—and put it on the desk of each person, where it would be totally accessible and readily usable. So Apple pressed ahead without undue concern about costs and probable sales, got the device to market, and created a new industry. Xerox was left in the dust, because it lacked a vision."

"That's quite a story," Susan responded. "It's funny, because in a sense, Apple must still be following its original vision. I mean, they're still gaining in the marketplace by focusing on making the computer user-friendly."

"Right," said Charles.

"So can we create a vision?" Susan asked.

"We can try. And I think we should make it focus on the consumer, like Apple did."

"How about, 'It's no hassle to buy, and a pleasure to own'? I think I heard something like that from some other company once."

"It's good, but what does it mean?"

"Well, it's customer-centered, and it means that if customers can buy from us easily and like what they purchase, then they'll come back to buy from us again."

"Okay. Any others?" Charles asked.

"Well, frankly, the one I really like is this: 'Our aim is to be the store the customer chooses.'"

"That means to do whatever is necessary to win the customer's loyalty?"

"Yes."

"That's good," Charles remarked.

"Do you like it?"

"Yes. I really do. Although, maybe I have one reservation."

Susan's face fell. "What is it?"

"I think a good vision should somehow be achievable, and that after it is achieved, it should become a routine objective. For example, the effort to put a person on the moon was at first a vision, but when NASA accomplished it, it became an objective. So yesterday's vision is today's objective, and we have to develop a new vision for the future. That's why I'm a little uncomfortable with the evergreen vision."

"What?" Susan asked.

"The evergreen vision, the one that never goes out of fashion—like aiming to be the store the customers choose. You'll always be pushing that idea, so you can't follow it with something new when time and overexposure lessens its impact."

"So I have to do some more work on a vision?"

"You might want to do it with your staff," Charles suggested, "and even include your rank-and-file employees. That way, everyone has an input and can feel that he or she owns the vision. I have a friend who runs a division at another company, and I remember him telling me what happened when he and a colleague from a different area of his company compared the visions that had been created for their divisions.

"'How could you issue this? It's full of grammatical mistakes,' his colleague challenged him. 'Mine is much more correct and readable.'

"'Who wrote yours?' my friend asked.

"'I did' was the reply.

"'Well,' my friend said, 'Mine was written by my whole organization. It took lots of time, and it isn't grammatically correct, but it's a living document that guides the actions of thousands of employees because they developed it and they believe in it. Who uses the one you wrote?'

"The answer was *no one*. It would sit on a shelf, contributing nothing to the business."

There was a pause in the conversation. Susan was absorbed in her thoughts.

"I also think that a vision should be exciting," Charles said, "so that it inspires and motives people. They should be able to point to the vision and say, 'We're proud to be part of that,' just as engineers who are trying to develop a new computer can say, 'Gee, you mean we can do that?'"

Susan nodded, but continued to think. After a few moments, she shared an observation: "Everything you've said so far about vision has focused on the business, not the organization; yet to many people a vision is about how people can work better together—about what kind of organization we can be."

"Yes, you're right," Charles replied. "I recognize that people can have a vision of how they want to work together—a vision of the culture of a firm—and that it's important. But we were discussing the management style you want to bring to your division, and I thought we were talking about vision for the business. After all, we've already discussed our vision for an empowered and fault-tolerant culture—we did that a couple of weeks ago. I do think organizational vision is important, but I thought we had covered it earlier and were on a different topic today."

"It's very important—it's a vision for the organization rather than for the business," Susan said. "And you're right, we did discuss it before. Let's move on."

"Do you want me to list some of the things we've been talking about?" Charles asked.

"Yes, please." Susan responded distantly, as if distracted by her thoughts.

So Charles recorded the most important points he had taken from their discussion. When he was finished, he suggested a break. The conference room's white board read:

A Vision

- *Is important for any business*
- *Should be achievable—but not easily*
- *Should be replaced by another after it's achieved*
- *Should have employee participation and buy-in from the outset*
- *Should be exciting in order to get people involved*

Chapter 8

The Fourth Step—*Setting Goals*

W hen they returned from their break, Susan said, "Let's move on. We have to talk about goals and missions."

"Well, 'mission statements,'" replied Charles, "if I correctly remember Doug's categories."

"Yes," Susan answered. "What do you remember about mission statements? I'm sorry I'm not carrying my part of the conversation today, but I'm thinking about my division while you talk. Is that okay?"

"Sure," Charles said, accepting his role for the morning.

"I think Doug would say that mission statements are not visions, but something different. They are also different from goals. Mission statements establish a set of values—'being the best at all we do, providing only top quality products, being the company everyone wants to work for'—or, as at IBM, assert the standards for the business—'the best service, the pursuit of excellence, respect for the individual.'

"I think mission statements are very useful. A vision focuses on what we want to achieve—or to be; a mission statement focuses on how we'll go about it. It should have several elements that reflect the primary concerns of the organization, including a customer-centered element, an employee-centered element, a community-centered element, and an investor-centered element. It should also express a company's values."

He went to the board and wrote:

A Good Mission Statement Includes Elements That Are

- *Customer-centered*
- *Employee-centered*
- *Investor-centered*
- *Community-centered*

And

It expresses the values of the firm.

"Also," Charles said as he wrote, "we should remember . . ."

Never confuse missions or goals with mission statements.

"I wrote this," he explained, "because what we have to do now is talk about how to develop the goals that will guide people in the division. We've talked about having a corporate vision or using your own substitute for one; about having a vision for the division; about stating our values in the form of a mission statement. Now we have to discuss the goals you must set if you're to empower people. Remember why we're doing this: we're trying to adopt a new management style that will cut our costs, improve the quality of our services, and enhance our responsiveness to our customers. It will enable us to achieve more with fewer people and resources, and if we're lucky, it will create a more fulfilling environment for all of us in the organization."

Susan agreed.

"So how do we set goals for our empowered teams?" Charles asked rhetorically. "Let's make a list." He wrote:

Characteristics of Well-Formulated Goals for Teams

"First," Charles began, "I'd say that goals should be understandable to those for whom they're prepared, and that means they can't all be financial. I went to a program for executives at a university once, and I was amazed how so many of the participants had such a shallow understanding of financial matters. Most of them pretended they were knowledgeable about the numbers, but they really weren't. In fact, getting up to speed on financial concepts seems to be one of the biggest reasons why companies pay to send their managers back to school. I mean, learning to read balance sheets and income statements is a key reason people get MBAs. But often in companies we just assume any given manager is sophisticated about financial measures, so we set up complex goals. It's counterproductive if a manager can't understand them."

He wrote on the board:

- *Understandable*

When he'd finished, he looked at Susan expectantly, as if it were her turn to suggest something for the board.

She hesitated a moment, then said, "Well, we're trying to develop the GEM management style, and we know that getting the goals right is a crucial element, right?"

Charles nodded in agreement.

"Then we should make sure of two things, at least," she continued. "First, we should ensure that the goals of the team are broad enough to serve as the basis for real empowerment of the team; and second, we should ensure that they are measurable. If we do these two things, then we have the basis for GEM management—goals, empowerment, and measurement. If we don't, if the goals are too narrow, then we can't practice empowerment; and if the results aren't measurable, then we can't know if the team succeeds or fails."

"Excellent points," Charles said with a high measure of respect in his voice. "Those are the basic things." He wrote:

- *Broad enough to support empowerment*

- *Narrow enough so that attainment can be measured*

87

"What else?" he asked Susan.

"Goals should have a time dimension. When should the result be accomplished? Do I have forever, or is the schedule very tight?"

Charles wrote:

- *Include a time dimension*

Susan looked at Charles expectantly. "Your turn," she said.

Charles stated, "Goals should be achievable, and they should be aligned with other activities in the organization—neither conflicting with them nor overlapping them." He wrote:

- *Achievable*
- *Aligned with other activities in the organization*

"I don't know about their not conflicting or overlapping," Susan objected. "It seems a nice point, but sometimes competition within an organization is a good idea. Isn't that the management style our CEO sometimes uses, when he puts two departments on the same issue and waits to see which comes up with the better solution?"

"Yeah, and what a mess it usually is," Charles said. "I've been involved in some of those situations. When one group finds out about the other, all kinds of rivalry, deception, and wasted effort develop as each tries to edge out the other. So I firmly maintain that teams shouldn't have conflicting or overlapping goals."

"Okay," Susan said, "I get your point, but don't write it up because I'm not sure I agree. I do agree on alignment, however, because without it the organization will work at cross-purposes."

"I have an idea," Charles suddenly burst out. "Our boss gave you a goal—or rather, a *mission,* to use Doug's preferred term. Let's check it out against our criteria for a proper set of goals. What did he tell you? I forgot."

"I've been thinking about that," Susan admitted, "and what he told me doesn't really fit the list we've developed. He told me to straighten out the division. So, is it understandable? Probably I understand it, but it isn't very detailed. What does 'straighten out' mean? Does it mean cut costs, improve efficiency, build revenue, reduce problems, build a competitive advantage? All of the above? I don't know.

"Next, is it broad enough for empowerment? It certainly is. Is it measurable? I don't think so—it's not specific enough to be measured. It's very subjective. My boss will look at what I've done and say 'It's okay' or 'It's not okay.' It'll be too subjective for me, I know.

"Does it include a time dimension?" she continued. "No. Is it achievable? Well, it depends on what it is that I'm expected to achieve. Is it aligned with other activities in the organization? Maybe. I wasn't told what else was happening that might affect what I do with the division."

"You sure didn't hit many of the criteria, did you?" Charles asked.

"You mean our boss didn't," Susan corrected him.

"Why don't you go back to him and try to clarify the goals?" Charles suggested. "You'd be a lot more comfortable."

"Maybe I will," Susan mused. "Maybe I will."

They ended their meeting.

After several days had passed, Charles received a call from Susan asking him to come to her office.

"I had a talk with our boss about my assignment to the retail division," she told him. "I tried to clarify what my goals were, as we discussed at our last meeting."

"Oh?" Charles responded, his eyes lighting up with interest.

"Yes, and he was very receptive. What we came up with is the following: I'm to increase sales by fifteen percent, and I'm to lower the costs of our goods sold through new suppliers by using better negotiating tactics and/or new distribution efficiencies.

"I have a year to achieve this, and I'll discuss progress quarterly with my boss. He did one other thing I liked."

"What?" Charles asked.

"He had me repeat the goals so we were sure that he and I both had the same understanding of them."

"Sounds good," said Charles. "Do the goals meet all our criteria?"

Susan shrugged.

"Let's see," Charles began. "Is it understandable?"

Susan nodded affirmatively.

"Is it broad enough for empowerment?" he asked. "Yes," he quickly answered his own question. "Is it measurable? Yes. Does it include a time dimension? Yes. Is it achievable?" He looked at Susan for an answer.

She replied, "I guess so, but it'll be difficult—a real stretch."

"But that's appropriate," Charles said. "Is it aligned with other activities in the organization?"

"Again," Susan said, "we didn't discuss that. I'll have to ask around."

"Still, it sounds like a pretty good set of goals. Let's check the whole situation against the basic conditions for empowerment that we set up in our first meeting. Do you know the goals? Yes. Do you have the information to make the right decisions?"

"I think I will," said Susan.

"Do you have competent people?"

"Yes."

"Are you prepared to make decisions and risk an error?"

"That's the problem," Susan said. "I don't think our culture is fault-tolerant. I'm afraid that if anything goes wrong, I'm in trouble."

"So what are you going to do?" Charles asked.

"Be very careful," Susan said, laughing. "I'm going to check out everything in advance."

"Then the company doesn't benefit much from empowerment—you'll be tying our boss up just as if he were micro-managing you."

"Yes, but I don't really have any choice in this culture, do I?" Susan said harshly, a note of belligerence creeping into her voice for the first time.

"No, I guess not," Charles conceded.

He turned to the whiteboard, on which still remained the list of items they had produced in their last meeting. He added at the bottom the two lessons of their previous conversation:

Always practice to get missions right.
Always have empowered persons repeat the
mission to ensure they understand it.

"That's very good, Charles," Susan told him, but her brow was furrowed and she seemed deep in thought. Her expression surprised Charles. He had thought the topic of goals was closed for the moment, but now he suspected she was about to open it back up.

"What are you thinking about?" he asked her.

"It occurred to me," Susan answered, "that we've been talking only about managers. We've talked about setting goals—what the company wants to accomplish—but what do the people get out of this? We can't think only about the managers."

Charles thought for a moment, then responded, "You're absolutely right. We've been focusing too much on the business and losing sight of the people."

"In some ways, that's all right," she said, continuing to muse about the matter. "We know that in an empowered environment people are likely to associate more fully with the firm's objectives, because the objectives become their own."

"Yes, but only if they're in on the successes," Charles objected. "It's a cop-out to say that we don't have to think about the people because empowerment will involve them."

"I agree," Susan said. "When we're preparing goals for the employees to benefit the firm, we should also consider how beneficial those goals will be for employees."

"Okay," said Charles, still standing beside board, "shoot!"

Susan gave him a sharp glance, as if to ask why it was her responsibility to make the suggestions, but she controlled her irritation and thought about a response.

"We have to pay people fairly," she began.

"More than that," Charles corrected her, "we have to pay them well by the standards of our industry and our community—if they perform well. We're asking more of them, and we have to pay them for it if the achievements are really there. I don't think of GEM as simply another form of exploitation—it's intended to improve the financial side for both the company and the employees."

"I agree," Susan said. "But we also have to treat people fairly. That's not easy even when we have well-trained supervisors, because the pressures of the business are always tempting people to take shortcuts."

"And," Charles interjected, "because people are always finding ways to squeeze a little more out of someone else."

Susan nodded. "It'll also be more difficult with the teams, since we won't be able to closely supervise people. There'll be tendencies for some on the teams to take advantage of others."

"But won't that just be team member against team member?" Charles protested. "It won't be the company being unfair to anyone."

"Of course it will," Susan said. "The teams are part of the company and are acting on its behalf. We have to train people to treat others fairly, we have to have a code of ethics which demands fair treatment, and we have to have a grievance or complaint mechanism to protect anyone who feels aggrieved."

"I guess so," Charles said, and he added on the board:

Rewards for Team Members
- *Good pay*
- *Fair treatment*

"What else?" Charles asked.

"It's very important that GEM provide greater opportunities for people. There won't be as many promotion ladders because we've delayered, so people will be concerned about the growth of their careers being stunted. We have to offset that."

"How?" Charles asked, feeling like Susan's student.

"We have to have good jobs in the teams," she answered. "We've already said they must have good earnings opportunities—"

"Hey," Charles interrupted her. "I like that." He turned to the board, crossed out "Good pay," and wrote in beside it:

- *Good earnings opportunities*

"It is a broader, better concept," Susan agreed. "And the jobs must have variety, interesting people to interact with, and the opportunity to learn and grow. We won't have much of a promotion ladder, but we can give people better assignments with more earnings opportunity. Finding good rewards for people is going to be a key part of management's tasks in the GEM system, I think."

Charles added to the list:

- *Interesting assignments*

"Is that it?" Charles asked.

"What do you think?"

"Does it seem like enough?"

"Well, it isn't unless we're able to make the company successful enough to provide some employment security for people," Susan responded.

"Yes," Charles agreed, " and that would help us with building trust too—what was it, the third, highest level of trust? Mutuality?"

"Yes, it was mutuality."

Charles wrote:

- *As much employment security as possible*

"Add one more thing," Susan suggested.

"What?"

"Achievements—accomplishments."

"Yes," Charles smiled, "and yet one more: a company of which to be proud." He wrote:

- *Accomplishments*

- *A company of which to be proud*

Charles took a look at the board. Once again they'd filled it with the results of their discussion.

A Good Mission Statement Includes Elements That Are

- Customer-centered
- Employee-centered
- Investor-centered
- Community-centered

And

It expresses the values of the firm.

Never confuse missions or goals with mission statements.

Characteristics of Well-Formulated Goals for Teams

- Understandable
- Broad enough to support empowerment
- Narrow enough so that attainment is measurable
- Include a time dimension
- Achievable
- Aligned with other activities in the organization

Always practice to get missions right.
Always have empowered persons repeat the mission to be sure they understand it.

Rewards for Team Members

- *Good earnings opportunities*
- *Fair treatment*
- *Interesting assignments*
- *As much employment security as possible*
- *Accomplishments*
- *A company of which to be proud*

Chapter 9

The Fifth Step—*Measurement*

"We really need to discuss measurement," Susan told Charles at their next meeting in the conference room. "It's the third element of the GEM style."

"I've been reluctant to bring up the subject," Charles admitted sheepishly.

"So have I," Susan said with a rueful grin.

"I think you're right, though," he said. "It's something we need to cover."

Her expression turned thoughtful. "Why do you think we've been so hesitant to work on measurement?"

"It's somewhat boring," Charles replied, "and complicated."

"Those are good reasons," Susan laughed. "But we've got to do it, so where do we start?"

"Actually, I've started already," he said with a smile. "I did some reading. I think I understand the types of measurement we need and the theory behind them, but I'd like to see the theory in action."

"What types do we need?" Susan asked.

"I'll put them on the chart and explain."

He positioned himself at the flip chart and began: "The way I see it, there are four types of measurement we need: financial, market-driven, operational, and organizational. All four are necessary because we not only want to know how well an empowered team is doing with respect to its goals, but we also want to provide the team with sufficient feedback so that it can effectively manage its own activities. This feedback ideally would take the form of continuing quantitative measures. So, although measuring team performance against team goals is the most important measurement, teams may have a more difficult time moving toward those goals if that's the only measurement we use.

"Now let's go through the types one by one."

He wrote on the chart:

- *Financial*

"These are measures of sales, costs, profits—if the unit is a profit center—investment levels, assets, even rates of return if possible." He paused. "We need measurements of expenditures against budgets, and of trend lines on all these things. On this item, as on each of the others, we'll need measures of performance against plan."

He waited a few moments, until Susan gestured for him to continue, and then added to the chart:

- *Market-driven*

"We want to know how well a team or other unit of the firm satisfies its customers, so we need market-share information. This requires measures of customer satisfaction, customer retention, and customer evaluations of our units against their competition. If the team has customers outside the firm, then these measures are obvious; but for our units that don't deal with the outside world, we have to identify internal customers so that measurements can be developed for them."

"I think," Susan interjected, "that we should also have measures of what our suppliers and vendors think of us. We need the cooperation of our suppliers, and we would want to know when we're trying to eke out profits by squeezing them too much."

"Good idea," Charles agreed.

He turned back to the chart. "Third, we want measures about our operations," he said as he wrote:

- *Operations*

"These measures include productivity, other efficiency measures, quality measurements, and turnaround times. They also include schedules and budgets and whether or not we're meeting them."

"Finally," he said, "we need organizational measures. These are the softest, I think, but are very important. How flexible is the team when there are changes in its goals, inputs, schedules, and so forth? How innovative is it? How effectively do the members work together? We need to develop measures of teamwork and of turmoil."

Charles recorded the last of his categories:

- *Organizational*

Susan looked at the chart quizzically, then shook her head. "There are a lot of measurements."

"Yes," Charles replied, "but if you can't measure it, you can't manage it—remember?"

"Oh, I know. But putting together all those measurements and maintaining them will be quite an effort. Do I really need all that for my division?"

"If you intend to do an outstanding job, you'll need them all, won't you?" Charles asked.

"I don't know," Susan resisted.

"Don't you already try to know something about each of these categories?" he asked. "You have to have the financials."

Susan nodded her head in agreement.

"And we've all learned in the past few years how crucial it is to look at our customer's attitudes toward us, right?"

Again Susan nodded.

"We need the operational measures—we can't let either efficiency or quality go unnoticed, and we have to measure both to really know what's happening, right?"

"Yes."

"So, the only new measures, if they are new, are the organizational measures."

She nodded again.

"But we've learned that when you look at the long-term, sustained performance of a division or a firm, or even a team, it's the innovativeness and the effective teamwork in the organization that determines its success, right? Consequently, we need to be aware of these things, and as systematically as possible, so that neither we nor the teams are under any illusions about how effective the teams really are as a group of people."

"I agree," Susan said, shaking her head in exasperation. "But it still seems like a lot to deal with."

"It is," Charles acknowledged. "But I don't see how we can operate in today's business climate without checking ourselves on each of these dimensions. It's too competitive and too fast-moving out there. Actually, we've been watching these things for several years now, and we're getting more sophisticated about it. That's why the measurements are important."

"But we don't have all those measurements today," Susan objected. "And come to think of it, our accounting system won't give us many of them, even on costs. Currently we can't even allocate costs to the different teams I'm setting up."

"I know that's a problem," Charles said sympathetically, "and I have an idea. It would be helpful for us both to see measurements in action. The other day I heard that a nearby manufacturing plant is using empowered teams. I know it's in manufacturing and not retail sales, which your division handles, but management there has been working on the matters we're discussing, and I think speaking with their operations manager would give you some ideas. I've made an appointment for us next week. Can you go?"

"I'm awfully busy," Susan demurred.

"You're going to tell me that you're so busy running the business that you don't have time to think about how to run it better?" Charles asked, teasing her.

Susan gave him a searching look, then realized she couldn't ignore the worth of his suggestion. "I'll try to join you," she conceded.

Several days later Susan and Charles arrived at the plant, which was quite small and fit in well with its suburban environment. They were ushered into a small conference room at the front of the plant, where they were briefed on its history.

"We're a vanishing breed in this country," Sheryl Smithland, the operations manager of the plant, told them. "Our plant does electronic-board assembly work, and most of this kind of work has gone to lower wage areas like Mexico and Southeast Asia.

But, by continually improving our productivity, we keep some two hundred jobs here.

"Almost a decade ago I introduced teams to improve quality— I guess I borrowed from the quality circle concepts of the Japanese—and over the years we've turned those advisory groups into fully empowered teams, and now they run their own activities. We have only two supervisors in the plant. With myself included, we have three management personnel for the two hundred workers in the factory. You can imagine that we in management don't direct the work closely—there are too few of us. The teams run production themselves."

Sheryl paused, then looked directly at Susan. "I was told that you were especially interested in the measurements we use—the ones that are team-specific. Is that right?"

"Yes," Susan answered.

"Then let's go out on the plant floor and take a look around," she suggested.

As they put on safety glasses and headed onto the plant floor, Sheryl explained: "Five years ago, after a year of preparation, each team was given a specific budget. Then we began the process of measuring performance against the budget. Teams were given a chart of monthly performance against budget and budget targets to hang at their work stations."

Sheryl stopped at a bulletin board. "Here's one," she said. "This belongs to the 'Classy Chassis' team."

"How many people are in the team?" Susan carefully interrupted.

"Seven," Sheryl responded, then continued her thought. "They've had these charts for several years, and recently we've added these others." She pointed to graphs that were pinned to a bulletin board just behind a work table. "This is a productivity chart showing the number of units per day, and this is a quality chart showing the number of rejects per day. With these charts the team can monitor its progress daily.

"We in management come through the plant every two weeks to review the charts and to make comments. I carry stickers and attach them to the charts when they fit. See, here's one. It reads,

'Great job!' Here's another. Because this team had some set-backs, I put this sticker on: 'Try harder next time.'" She smiled.

Several of the team's members came over and greeted Sheryl, who then introduced them to their visitors. They listened, nodding in agreement from time to time as she continued to tell Charles and Susan about the plant and the teams.

"The team members are responsible for arranging and scheduling their own tasks—with the help of a team-elected leader. The team does the actual production work as well as the administrative duties, such as training, inventory and scrap control, housekeeping, and quality assurance. We provided team members with financial training so that they would understand how budgets are prepared. This training has paid off, as they often have to fill in a cost report or do a quality control assignment."

"How long did it take to get the measurements set up?" Charles asked.

Two team members grinned at each other. Sheryl nodded at them. "How long?" she asked.

"Too long," one responded.

Sheryl laughed. "What Joe means is that the teams were waiting for the measurements for a long time before we got them done. Actually, this was in some ways the most difficult and most time-consuming task we had to complete in order to get the plant operating fully on an empowered-team basis. Our accounting system couldn't distinguish among the teams, and we had to have costs, productivity, and quality data for each one."

"It makes it a lot easier to run the team when we know what's actually happening," Joe explained. "Before we had the charts, it was as if we were flying blind."

Later, as they were preparing to leave, Charles asked Sheryl a final question: "How's the plant doing?"

She gave him a serious glance. "Competition is brutal," she replied, "but we're holding our own well enough that the company wants to double employment in the plant."

"That's wonderful!" Charles responded, congratulating her.

"I don't know. It's difficult to expand a plant with empowered teams that quickly," Sheryl told him. "We have to teach everyone who comes in how to work in this environment, and we have to give them training in the financial and scheduling skills they'll need, to say nothing of technically teaching them their new jobs. So it will be quite a challenge." She paused for thought, then added, "But I wouldn't change it. If we weren't using this system, we wouldn't be here. There'd be no jobs here at all."

The next day, back at his office, Charles added to the charts on his easel the list of measurements he had recorded the previous day in the conference room. The new page briefly read:

Measurements

- *Financial*
- *Market-driven*
- *Operational*
- *Organizational*

Chapter 10

The Sixth Step—*Motivation*

"I was thinking over what Doug Royal told us," Charles told Susan at their next encounter. "Suddenly I realized what empowerment means for motivation. It has changed motivation entirely!"

"What do you mean?" Susan asked. "How can it change motivation?

"Think about it," Charles encouraged her. "What is it that we want employees to do? What is it that we are trying to motivate them to do? In the ODS system we want them to follow the directions given by their supervisors. The idea is that the supervisor is acting on behalf of the firm, and if the employees will just obey the supervisor, then everything will work out fine for the firm. The supervisor is concerned about minimizing costs and improving quality, so the theory goes; consequently, if the employee will just obey, then the right things will get done.

"And yet, we know that often this isn't the case. Employees may know more about how to cut costs and improve quality than their supervisors.

"Nonetheless, that's what motivation has meant: getting employees to follow the dictates of their supervisors in whatever way possible. And managers have been trained in how to get employees to obey. There are rewards for obedience and punishments for disobedience. All sorts of manipulative techniques have been tried.

"Most of them aren't working very well, however. The whole culture of today's world is saying no. Schools, peers, the media, rock music—all of them tell today's individual that he or she should be independent—that authority isn't to be trusted. Nowhere is obedience glorified, or even endorsed; it isn't a virtue today. So when a company tries to motivate its people to obey their supervisors, it's fighting a very difficult uphill battle.

"But the GEM system changes that. No longer do we want the employee to obey; instead, we ask him or her to internalize the company's objectives directly—to care about cutting costs, improving quality, and enhancing responsiveness to customers. We ask the employee to adopt these objectives as her or his own and to do whatever is possible to make them a reality.

"We've dropped the middle person. That's the motivation revolution—and it is a revolution. We no longer depend on the supervisor or manager to pursue cost-cutting, improve quality, and enhance customer response, and only depend on the employee to obey the supervisor. Now we ask the employee to do directly what the supervisor used to tell him or her to do.

"When I think about this," Charles continued, "I recall a story about T.E. Lawrence, better known as 'Lawrence of Arabia.' During World War I, he did what no European had ever been able to do before: assemble an Arab army and get it to march successfully against the Turks. When he was asked how he did it, he replied, 'People who cannot be driven at all can sometimes very easily be led.' What he meant was that European-style discipline was of no use at all with people as independent as the Arabs, so all those Europeans who'd tried to drive the Arabs to military exertion had failed. But fighters as independent, proud, and effective as the Arabs could be led into battle by a committed European. This is what Lawrence had done.

"Today's employees are like the Arabs whom Lawrence led: they are independent, proud, and effective. They resist being driven by supervisors and managers, but they are prepared to be led by those who will work with them. The GEM style is like Lawrence's method, mobilizing the people by demonstrating personal commitment and showing others how to be successful against the enemy—or the competition, as the case may be.

"So we motivate in the GEM fashion by helping our empowered teams understand how important cost-cutting, quality improvement, and customer responsiveness are to their success. We then step aside and let them do it. It's brilliant, I think. It explains why today GEM can obtain so much greater performance from employees than ODS: GEM fits the people."

Charles went to the flip chart and wrote in an excited hand:

The Motivation Revolution

ODS

> *Motivates people to obey the supervisor or manager, who cares about cost-cutting, quality improvement, and customer responsiveness.*

GEM

> *Motivates people to care about cost-cutting, quality improvement, and customer responsiveness.*

Susan smiled at Charles, but with a measure of tolerance. Over the months of their discussions he'd become increasing enthusiastic about the new management style. In contrast, she still had major reservations. She voiced one now.

"That's all to the good, but not everyone in an empowered team is going to really care about cost-cutting and all that. Without supervisors, who's to see that those people make a contribution?"

"You underestimate the impact of peer pressure within the empowered teams," Charles responded. "You went to business school, didn't you?"

"Yes," Susan replied.

"Did you have a study group in which you participated?"

"Yes."

"Remember how it was? If you hadn't participated in that study group, would you have been as committed to the reading required in the curriculum? I doubt it. If you hadn't done all the reading, you might not have been able to answer a question in class. Not much of a penalty. But in the study groups, a loyalty to one another built up, which caused us to feel an obligation to fulfill our part in completing our assignments. If I didn't do my share, then my group mates would be embarrassed in class, and that made me work. In the executive education program I recently attended, the instructors didn't even give any grades, but still we worked. Why? Because of our study teams.

"I think an individual's performance is, in most cases, the direct result of a basic personal need to contribute to the good of the whole and to receive recognition for that contribution. Very few of us are prepared to let down our partners if we can avoid it.

"So this is the motivational genius of the empowered teams. It gives the team a substantial set of goals and the freedom to pursue them as it sees fit; and by involving individuals in a team, it uses peers to drive performance by all those involved. Teamwork, delegation, and empowerment are all designed for this purpose—to motivate people to internalize business goals. Finally, GEM management says to the team, 'Go after the primary purposes—cut costs, improve quality, enhance responsiveness—and don't be diverted to secondary purposes, such as obeying the directions of a boss.' It's marvelous, just marvelous!"

"Don't get carried away," Susan admonished him.

"Do you think I'm wrong?" Charles asked.

She replied slowly, considering her words carefully. "No. I hadn't seen as clearly as you the connection between the individual and the team in the motivation area."

Charles added to the chart so that under the GEM heading it read:

Motivates people to care about cost-cutting, quality improvement, and customer responsiveness via teamwork.

"There's something else I've been thinking about," Charles offered hesitantly. "Can I mention it, or have I been talking too much?"

"You've been talking a lot," Susan told him, smiling, "but go on."

"I came across a story about a coach who had a team that was about to play a big game. But in the weeks before the game, a number of the team's best players had been injured and were still unable to play. The press learned of the lost players and awarded the game in advance to the other team.

"On the morning of the big game, the coach met in the locker room with the team. Do you know what he did?"

"I haven't a clue," Susan answered.

"Well, what would you have done?"

"I hate sports examples."

"Oh, come on. What would you have done?" Charles pressed her.

"I suppose I'd have said something about our having played well all season and not having anything to lose now—because so little was expected of us—but having a great deal to win," she said.

"And?"

"Oh, I'd have said that even though we were without key players, we had some advantages: our substitutes would be highly motivated; the other team might be overconfident, and even off-guard about any new plays and players we might have."

"Very good," said Charles. "More?"

"I guess I'd end by saying that we had a great opportunity and should go out to win the game." Susan finished her statement with a decisive nod.

"That's great!" Charles enthused. "You'd be a great coach."

"So what did I learn from that?" Susan asked. "What was your point?"

"Well," Charles began with a triumphant grin, "the actual coach did all that you suggested, but he also did one more thing. As he approached the end of the meeting, with the game looming just ahead, he said to the team: 'In my family we have a tradition. When a family member does something really good, we gather after dinner in the living room and, going in sequence, give our personal reasons for why we should be very proud of what the person accomplished and why we're glad the person is in the family. We have to be sincere.

"'Now,' the coach continued, 'I want each of you to pick out another person on our team and tell that person why you are proud

109

to be on the same team with him and what you're going to do to support him in the game we're about to play.'

"So," Charles continued, "they went around the room praising each other and committing themselves to support one another. You can imagine that as they did so, they build a tremendous bond of emotion with one another. They went out to play the game and won what is probably the most amazing upset in the history of the sport."

Susan was listening intently.

"You see," Charles began to explain, "most coaches would do what you did: give the team a speech. But in the end, the coach can't motivate the team; the team must motivate itself. In the same way, a supervisor can't really motivate the employees; they must motivate themselves. The task of a manager in an empowered team environment is the same as that of a coach: to create conditions that will help the team motivate itself. Managers in the GEM system are called upon not just to give speeches, but to provide a setting in which teams can motivate themselves and to devise imaginative opportunities that encourage team self-motivation. Few teams can do this for themselves, and this is what is necessary for outstanding team performance."

"That's an impressive lesson," Susan admitted. "I really hadn't seen that at all."

"Probably because we're all so locked in the old ODS mode of thinking that we don't really understand what GEM requires of us," Charles commented.

He wrote on the chart:

Maxims of Motivation

- *A team must motivate itself.*
- *The coach must create the settings.*

"I feel like you've done all the work today," Susan said. "But I do have one thing to contribute. I've been reading about some of the research on motivation that has recently been conducted in Europe, and I picked up something important. I always thought that a satisfied employee was a motivated employee, but often that's not the case. It's obvious if you think about it. Some people are satisfied with their jobs because the jobs demand so little of them.

"'I've got the best job in the world,'" Susan play-acted in a shrill voice. "'I don't have to do anything at all at work.'"

Charles laughed.

"Job satisfaction may be fine for keeping complaints down and unions out," Susan continued, "but it's not motivation. What the Europeans did was study actual job performance, and they found that high performance—motivation turned into action—was rooted in excitement about the job. And what is job excitement? It's a feeling that the work is important and significant; that a person will be given recognition for success; that's there's variety in what is done, as well as with whom a person works; and that a person is involved with others who are also excited about the work."

"That's amazing, but it makes sense," Charles remarked. "So we have several factors contributing to motivation: teamwork, empowerment, and job excitement."

"You see," Susan told him, "we don't want satisfaction—we want creative dissatisfaction associated with excitement about the job. That's what motivation is made of."

"What a great summary!" he exclaimed. "I get so tired of hearing people in this profession talk about employees as if they were ICBUs."

"ICBUs?" Susan asked.

"Interchangeable carbon-based assets," Charles explained. He went to the flip chart and wrote:

- *Job excitement is the key to motivation.*

Susan followed him, and added:

- *Don't presume people are motivated.*

- *Don't accept less than full commitment.*

- *Always build excitement.*

111

On the board the two had written:

> ### The Motivation Revolution
>
> **ODS**
>
> > Motivates people to obey the supervisor or manager, who cares about cost-cutting, quality improvement, and customer responsiveness.
>
> **GEM**
>
> > Motivates people to care about cost-cutting, quality improvement, and customer responsiveness via teamwork.
>
> ### Maxims of Motivation
>
> - A team must motivate itself.
> - The coach must create the setting.
> - Job excitement is the key to motivation.
> - Don't presume people are motivated.
> - Don't accept less than full commitment.
> - Always build excitement.

Chapter 11

Empowering

"It seems strange," Susan told Charles, "that we should come to the topic of empowerment at this late a date in our discussions. This is where we started—talking about taking more initiative ourselves and giving others the chance to take it. We began with empowerment, then talked about everything else. Why was that?"

"Good question," Charles responded. "I think it may have been Doug Royal who sent us in this direction. Didn't he tell us that empowerment had to be accompanied by goals and measurement, and that empowerment was the easiest of the three to accomplish? Didn't he say that if we set the stage properly, most people would accept empowerment?"

"I don't remember who came to that conclusion," Susan said, "but I hope it's right. We've spent a lot of time setting the stage, and it's time for us to talk about empowerment directly."

"I agree," replied Charles. "First, what is empowerment?"

"That's easy," Susan offered. "It's giving more authority and autonomy to people in their work."

"But as part of the GEM management system, it means something more specific," Charles contended. "It means allowing people considerable discretion in how they pursue business goals."

"Are we talking about empowering teams or individuals?"

"I think teams, mostly," Charles responded, "and individuals within the teams."

"You don't expect each individual in a team to have separate goals and measurements, do you?" Susan asked incredulously.

"No, I don't. That's a good point. The individual is empowered because the team is empowered, but the individual isn't free to go off on his or her own.

"But actually, Susan," Charles continued, "there are several versions of empowerment: we can empower teams, thereby empowering the people in them; we can empower an executive or manager who leads a department, although he or she might not empower people who work in the department; or we can empower an individual who works largely independent of others."

"Yes, I understand that," Susan said. "We have some options." She paused. "But the big issue is this: Do people want to be empowered?"

"Not everyone, certainly," Charles responded. "And the fewer the people who want empowerment, the less we have established the right conditions for empowerment. But I think that when the stage is set correctly, most people will want it.

"The other day one of my old-time employees made a memorable comment when we were discussing giving people much more responsibility in their work. She told me, 'It sounds like we're all finally growing up in the workplace—we're being treated like adults, given the freedom to make our own decisions.'

"She had a valid point, and after our discussion I thought about it for quite some time. We allow adults to make life-and-death decisions about their lives, and sometimes about the lives of others, but in business we say they can't act without approval. Why not? I asked myself. The answer was all too clear: because money is involved, and we're afraid that if a person makes the wrong decision, we'll lose some money. People can make decisions about having children, about what to do with their lives, even about owning weapons, but when it comes to money in the workplace, *we* say they have to have permission. No wonder people don't bring their best efforts to the workplace."

"Some companies have been raising the level of financial commitment people can make without upper-level approval," Susan commented.

"That's a step in the direction of empowerment," Charles said, "although real empowerment does more. It gives people resources—including financial resources—and the freedom to allocate them as they see best, in order to attain the goals they have accepted."

"I don't think many people want that degree of responsibility," Susan insisted. "When people are empowered, they become responsible not just for doing what they're told, but for deciding what to do and for the consequences. That's a result of empowerment, and it scares many people."

"It makes much more effective business people of them," Charles replied, "at whatever level or function they have in the firm."

"I agree, but not everyone wants to be more effective. Many people just want to do what they're told and then go home and forget work entirely."

"There's room in an empowered environment for such people," Charles said, "as long as there aren't too many of them. For example, an empowered team can absorb some people who just want the rest of the team to tell them what to do. And in any team, some people are likely to be prepared to take more responsibility than others—so some can take very little if they wish. I don't think they should get as much reward when the team's successful, but they don't have to be driven out."

Susan looked at him as if she wasn't sure she agreed.

Charles defended his point. "I think this is important. We shouldn't confuse the purity of our theory about empowerment with the somewhat messier reality. We would like to have an environment in which everyone accepts empowerment completely, but that's an illusion. Human institutions are never so perfect. Instead, we have a situation in which some people accept much more responsibility than others. Some welcome empowerment and thrive on the accountability. Others don't. However, that doesn't mean that we can't achieve much better business results by pushing ahead on empowerment."

"Maybe not," Susan said, unconvinced. Realizing they were at an impasse, she came at the subject from a new angle. "You keep talking about responsibility and accountability, but we have that in the old management systems—ODS(A) and ODS(P)—right? There's a big difference, though, in what those words mean in the empowered setting, isn't there?"

"You're very sharp with your questions today, aren't you?" Charles said in a challenging manner. For a few moments, he wondered how he could come up with a persuasive answer.

Finally he replied: "Yes, there is a big difference. It's funny. We have two different words that we use interchangeably, as if they were perfect synonyms: *responsibility* and *accountability*. This is unfortunate because we have two very different realities to describe. It would be nice to have one word for one reality and another word for the other reality. As it is, we have two words that refer to one reality and no word for the other reality. Crazy, huh?

Susan gave him a puzzled look.

"Let me explain," Charles said. "In the ODS systems—that is, in traditional directive management—responsibility is something imposed on a person. The boss deputizes someone to carry out a task and thereby places a clear, unambiguous responsibility on that person to do that task. We call that hierarchically imposed obligation both "responsibility" and "accountability." We say the person is responsible for doing that task and is accountable if it doesn't get done.

"But in an empowered environment, there is a larger concept of responsibility or accountability. A person accepts undivided accountability for the goals, shared with the other members of the empowered team. Unlike the traditional situation, in which the responsibility is imposed, here it must be accepted, bought into by the empowered person. It's something I accept rather than something imposed on me. The difference is significant, and it can have profound effects on how well people work together in a business.

"To go back to where I started, empowerment demands more of the individual than directive management, so we ought to have different words for the two different meanings. I like to say that directive management imposes *responsibility* on people, while GEM causes people to accept *accountability*. But it doesn't really matter how the words are applied as long as the distinction is clear."

"Very interesting, Charles," Susan said. "I think I see the difference. Still, that doesn't change the fact that many people

116

don't want to accept what you refer to as accountability in the empowered context."

"You have something very specific on your mind, don't you?" he asked.

Susan nodded in affirmation.

"What is it?"

"I just spent two days with the top management of the division I recently received," she began. "Many of them have been with the division for years—back when it was strong and doing well, and throughout its subsequent decline. I'd been studying the business, and I knew what our senior executives thought about it and what the consultants we've had study it have recommended. But I wondered, What do the people who've been running the business think about it? Do they have any ideas about how to revitalize it?

"So I took them off-site, where they wouldn't be distracted by phone calls and subordinates, and divided them into teams. Next, I assigned each team an aspect of the business and asked them to prepare a plan for revitalizing it. I had team members focus on the area of the business they ordinarily work in, so that the people actually running the business could decide what should be done about the area for which they have responsibility—or maybe accountability.

"I gave them most of the two days to meet together as groups and prepare recommendations. On the afternoon of the second day, I called them together as a whole, and we listened to reports from one group after another.

"By the time they were finished I was so angry, I felt as if I had to get out of the room before I said something I'd always regret."

"Were the reports that bad?" Charles asked. "Did they have no idea what to do with the business?"

"Not at all," Susan replied. "They had great ideas. They seemed to know just what was wrong and had excellent suggestions for what to do about it. Their ideas very closely tracked those of our top executives and the consultants—except these people were closer to actual operations and had a better grasp of the details."

117

"So they were great reports?"

"Great," Susan answered.

"Then why were you upset?" Charles asked.

"Because in every instance the people who prepared those reports already had all the authority they needed to make the changes they recommended. That's what upset me so. Why haven't they acted?"

"Wow!" Charles exclaimed. "Now I see what's troubling you. Your people have the authority to act—they're empowered, if you will—but they don't act. They just keep doing the same old things even though it's destroying the business."

"That's it," Susan said, her lips drawn tightly in exasperation.

"I've seen situations like that," Charles tried to reassure her. "You have to remember that although a person may know what needs to be done, he or she can't do it alone. They all may have the power to act, but no one person alone can change the system. Perhaps to you they seem to be empowered, but they aren't—at least not individually. They're probably supposed to be empowered as a team, but no one has made a team of them. Maybe they don't know how to work together well enough to trust each other to do his or her part, so they're stymied. Each person knows what to do, but can't do it alone, and because they aren't a team, they don't work together to get the changes made."

Susan's eyes got wide. "That could be right. Charles, that's amazing. You could be right."

"Amazing that I could be right? Or amazing what the problem is?"

Susan grinned. "Amazing what the problem is." She paused. "If you're right, why is the situation like this? Why can't they work together as a team?"

"Probably for several reasons," Charles conjectured. "There's a lot of stress when people accept accountability for big changes in the business. They may have tried and broken down under the load. I was talking to some of the team members in that factory you and I visited a while ago, and they told me how much head work there is. One fellow said, 'I was used to physical labor, but here there's lots of head work as well.' A woman told me, 'When I go home in the evening, I'm mentally tired. When we first started in these teams, I had to take tranquilizers to calm me down at night.' Another man told me he'd started drinking to deal with the stress. But all of them said that by working as a team and depending on one another, they had finally learned how to live with the accountability and their stress level had gone way down.

"I'll bet that your people don't know how to depend on each other, and so the stress level that comes from accepting accountability for big changes in the business is just too high."

Susan went to the chart and wrote:

Helping People with Empowerment

- Coping with stress

"Is there more?" she asked Charles.

"Yes," he smiled in answering. "If people are going to work closely together, they have to be able to give and take criticism in a constructive way. That's not at all easy. Most of your managers are undoubtedly very proud and don't like to be criticized. It's one thing to have the boss criticize us—even if we don't like it, we're prepared to accept it unless the criticism is too harsh—but it's another thing to have our peers criticize us. No one likes other people to get down on them. I'd wager that when your managers try to work as a team, they can't find a way to give or receive criticism without disrupting their relationships. And there has to be criticism, for how else can problems be identified and improved?"

Susan wrote:

- Giving and receiving constructive criticism

"What can I do about that?" she asked.

"You can address it directly in a team-building and training program. Team building isn't just getting to like each other, and it's not even just developing problem-solving abilities; it's very much learning to trust each other enough to accept criticism without getting angry at the person who gives it to you. So it's also learning how to give criticism in a nonthreatening and nonjudgmental way."

"Is that possible?"

"To a large degree, yes." Charles paused. "There's one more thing," he said. "Do you want to hear it?"

"Yes."

"I bet your people have trouble communicating."

"Not at all," Susan said. "Every one of them is very vocal."

"They're all good at speaking their minds?" Charles asked.

"Very good," she responded emphatically.

"How are they at listening?"

Susan looked at him in surprise. "I hadn't thought of that," she said.

"I suspect that every one of your people is prone to answering another without really listening to what the other person has said. And that can get them in a lot of trouble."

"I think you're right," Susan answered, adding to the list:

- *Learning to listen carefully*

"Is that all?" she asked Charles.

"Yes, except to say that you have to train people thoroughly so that they learn how to develop these skills to a high degree. These are the three key skills required by empowerment. They're not required to anywhere near the same degree in the ODS modes, so most people haven't perfected them; nonetheless, successful teamwork requires them, so you have to invest in training people."

"If I do that, do you think my people will accept empowerment?"

"If you train them to handle the stress, to give and accept constructive criticism, and to listen carefully to one another, then they'll act as an empowered team without any hesitation."

Susan nodded appreciatively and took a last glance at the chart.

Helping People with Empowerment
- *Coping with stress*
- *Giving and receiving constructive criticism*
- *Learning to listen carefully*

Chapter 12

Managing Change

"I've asked Doug Royal to join us again," Charles told Susan when they met a few days later in the conference room. "We're supposed to talk about change today, and Doug is more for that than anyone else I know."

"That's because he's the corporate gadfly," Susan responded, laughing and greeting Doug warmly.

A bit uncertain that he was being complimented, Doug hesitated and gave her a puzzled look, but he then returned her welcome with gusto.

"Doug," Charles began, "Susan and I have had several meetings since we last spoke with you. We've been trying to understand the GEM management system you introduced to us. Susan even has started transforming the division she's now heading into a new-style organization."

"I had to," Susan said. "They gave me bigger objectives than my predecessor and less people and resources to work with."

"That's what's happening all over," Doug responded. "So you're trying to step up the performance of the division?"

"I'm trying to reengineer it," Susan answered, smiling and savoring the jargon as it passed her lips.

Doug and Charles smiled.

"Anyway," Charles resumed, "we know pretty much where we want to end up and what techniques for effective management we can use once we get there, but we're wondering how we should manage the transition."

"Most of the people who work for me seem perfectly satisfied with things the way they've been," Susan explained. "I've talked to them about what we need to do—about the transformation to

121

GEM—and they're very reluctant. You know people, they just don't want to change."

"Yes," Charles added. "I guess we're all like that."

Susan and Charles did not seem to have any reservations about making these sweeping statements about human nature, evidently believing such generalities both self-evident and unobjectionable. They were therefore astonished when Doug seemed to get very upset.

"That's not human nature!" he burst out. "Not human nature at all!"

Taken aback, Susan and Charles bristled at his accusation—he'd as much as said they were not telling the truth.

Seeing a sudden hostility in their eyes, Doug caught hold of his emotions. "I'm sorry," he apologized quickly. "I didn't mean to get so agitated. It's just that whenever I hear that opinion—that it's human nature to resist change—I get all churned up inside."

"So I see," said Charles warily. "Why? It's human nature for people not to welcome change, isn't it?"

"I don't think that's human nature at all," Doug protested. "It may be how most people behave in the workplace, but it's not in their nature; it's due to the circumstances they find themselves in."

Charles and Susan exchanged a quizzical glance, which Doug saw and whose significance he grasped.

"Please let me try to explain," Doug said earnestly. "It might take a moment, but this is important."

Susan made a broad, sweeping motion with her hand, as if giving him the stage.

"Think about the matter systematically," he suggested. "Entertainment, travel, and fashion are among the world's greatest industries. People will pay them considerable amounts of money for novelty, diversion, and change.

"In the entertainment business, movie stars rise rapidly into popularity and decline just as quickly. People tire of them, so intense is the demand for something new. Not long ago, The New Kids On The Block were all the rage, but who has heard of them recently? When a music group repeatedly climbs to the top of the charts over a long period of time, we marvel at its staying power.

"You can see a similar need for novelty and change in the travel industry: travel agents promote one destination, then another; global travellers search out this exotic spot, then that; vacationers prefer one hotel today, and another tomorrow; people flock to a certain hot spot one season, then ignore it the next. As with entertainment and fashion, you can barely grasp the latest vogue before it's over.

"Styles in fashion are always in flux. The world of apparel is driven by experimentation with new fabrics, colors, and styles. The wealthy seek out unique creations and proudly wear them. Some people refuse to be seen wearing the same outfit twice. Change fuels this industry as well as entertainment and travel, and the need for change in these industries is reflective of society at large. Wherever we look, there's a premium on change—and people pay for its excitement."

He paused, his bright eyes conveying a sense of anticipation that more was to come.

Charles responded with raised eyebrows and a shrug, as if acknowledging that what Doug said was true, yet questioning its significance.

"Of course, wherever we look *except* in the office." Doug smiled mischievously. "There, we are continually told by others, and we continually tell ourselves, that people resist change. It's human nature to resist change, we say, especially as people grow older."

Doug threw out his arms in a theatrical gesture. "Are these the same people who go to movies for vicarious adventure, who read novels to experience someone else's life, who pay large sums for the latest recording of a band newly emerging into popularity, who study travel folders and guidebooks to find new places to visit? Can these possibly be the same people, behaving in such different ways in different settings?"

He looked intently at his two companions, waiting for them to answer. After a few moments of silence, he answered his own questions.

"Yes, in most instances, they are. The people in our offices who are well-known stick-in-the-muds are also customers for all sorts of diversion, believing it to be fun. When they step outside the office, those in our business who resist change suddenly undergo a transformation and willingly, even urgently, press money upon those who can sell them diversion and change. How can this be?"

Again Doug waited for a response and, getting none, resumed speaking.

"The answer is already evident, for to ask the right question is always to obtain an enlightening answer. These people are the same, and it's as much a part of their human nature to welcome change as to resist it."

Charles shook his head in grudging agreement. Susan sat without showing emotion.

"If human nature isn't to blame for the apparent rigidity of people in the business environment, then what is?" Doug asked.

Charles and Susan looked uncomfortably at each other, then at Doug, but neither spoke.

"It's because of the environment at work," Doug answered firmly, creating the impression that he was directing an accusation at his companions. "We make change so uncomfortable for people at work that they suppress their natural desire for novelty and diversion and hold rigidly to the status quo. Consequently, people who outside the workplace pay for change resist it vigorously in the workplace."

Charles responded defensively to the implied criticism in Doug's remarks. "You may say that people aren't really resistant to change, but others don't agree with you."

He reached into the top drawer of his desk and pulled out a sheet of paper.

"I've been so concerned about the question of how we get from our ODS management style to GEM," he said, "that I even copied down something I read in a management journal about it. I don't think you should criticize me—or Susan—as though we're to blame for our people's hesitancy to change. Listen to this . . ."

Holding up the paper, Charles read: "'People's inability to change . . . is the limiting factor in transforming organizations.'"*

---

*Robert I. Benjamin and Jon Blunt, "Critical IT Issues: The Next Ten Years," *Sloan Management Review,* Summer 1992, p. 16.

He then waved the paper toward Doug as if to say, "See, I'm right! It's not me who's causing the resistance—others have noted it too, and say it's widespread."

Doug smiled at Charles. "I didn't mean to blame you personally," he said in a conciliatory tone of voice. He extended his apology to Susan as well, with a nod of his head. "I just meant to say that all of us in management share part of the responsibility.

"As for the quotation you read, I know that's a very common view, even the prevalent view, but I think it's dead wrong—not only wrong, but pernicious. And if it is right, it reflects a common pathology in firms that is due not to the people, but to the setting in which management puts them. People aren't at all unable to change, but they are often unwilling—and we can change that!"

Doug looked intensely at Charles and Susan, who were now listening to him closely. "The reason people are unwilling to welcome change is that managers aren't smart about the psychology of change. It's simple, really. Managers allow a situation to occur in which change is accompanied by things people resist—specifically, risk and compulsion. So it isn't the change that's resisted, it's what accompanies it."

Doug went to the flip chart and wrote:

When Change Is Accompanied By

Risk

and

Compulsion

People Resist It.

"Now, we can minimize the degree of risk and compulsion that accompanies change, and if we do so, we can minimize the resistance of people to change. In fact, they will usually welcome it for the diversion and novelty it offers. I once studied people who had changed occupations in a company—not just jobs, but occupations—and so had to learn a whole new set of skills. Some resisted and some welcomed the transition. What explained the different reactions? Were they due to personality differences?

Personality did play a role to a degree, but only a small degree. The big difference was that some of the people saw the change as very risky for them but were compelled to go along with it; they resisted vigorously, and many never made the transition successfully. Others had been provided a safety net if the new occupation didn't go well—so the risk was much reduced in their minds—and had been allowed to volunteer for the change. They saw the change as an opportunity and welcomed it, reasoning, 'Why wouldn't I want to make the change? I might do much better in the new position, and if I don't, then I can go back to something similar to what I was doing before. There's no risk, and I might do better in the new position—of course I want to try it out.' And, as you might expect, those in this welcoming frame of mind did much better in the new situation.

"That's the psychology—and the paradox—of managing change. We usually manage change in a way that invites risk and compulsion, which isn't necessary and which causes people to resist the change, although actually it isn't the change they're resisting, it's the risk and compulsion.

"The risk is that if the new situation doesn't work out, they'll lose their career or their job, or both. That's enough to make anyone nervous and adverse to taking the risk. Then, as if that weren't enough, we force them into the change, force them into the risky situation. Any sensible person resists being compelled to do something risky; it's similar to being forced backwards toward the edge of a cliff—anyone resists. And, incredibly, in business this is how we try to manage change most of the time." Doug shook his head in wonderment as he finished speaking.

Charles and Susan sat silent, stupefied, as if a great light were dawning in their minds. Finally Susan spoke.

"If you're right," she said to Doug, "what can we do about it?"

"We can minimize risk, and we can eliminate compulsion," Doug answered directly and concisely. "We minimize risk by training and by providing a safety net. Training is crucial because empowered teams and GEM management are new to most people. They find the management style unfamiliar, and that makes them uncomfortable with it. To that extent, people are wary of change; they're cautious about the unknown. But that isn't the same as being resistant to change—not at all. If we provide training and a safety net, then the caution gives way to interest and excitement. People welcome change.

"The training we must provide has two elements. First, we have to help people understand the work content of what they'll be doing in the new setting. In an empowered environment, people have broader responsibilities, so there's a lot to learn. For example, in a factory people often have to learn the whole assembly line, including both the direct assembly work and many supporting functions. In some factories, direct assembly jobs are called 'horizontal tasks' and supporting activities are called 'vertical tasks.' Over time people must master both.

"The second element of training involves how to work in teams and cooperate effectively with other people. Specifically, people need to learn how to give and receive constructive criticism—"

Charles interrupted, "We've talked about that. We understand how important training is to making the new systems work."

"That's good," Doug responded. "I'm simply pointing out that if the training is comprehensive and done well, then it's a major factor in reducing resistance to change. Training enables the firm to kill two birds with one stone: first, it makes it possible for people to do a good job in the new setting, and second, it reduces resistance to the change. It's a great investment for a firm, and should be thought of as an investment, not treated as a cost to be minimized."

Charles and Susan nodded to one another in agreement, then watched as Doug wrote on the flip chart:

How to Reduce Resistance to Change

- *Eliminate the perception of risk*
    - *By training people well*

"We can also eliminate risk for people by providing a safety net for them," he said. "For example, we should tell a person that if he or she takes a new position or tries working on an empowered team, accepting the increased responsibility which that entails, then if it doesn't work out, she or he can go back to a more traditional setting. We won't always have the person's original job for him or her to return to, but we can find something similar to it.

"Now, I grant you, this could become a problem if we had too many people who wanted to take advantage of the safety net and go back to their original jobs, but that isn't likely, and that's the paradox I spoke of earlier. By offering people a safety net we minimize their resistance to change, and since they enter the new situation with a will to make it work and few reservations, they usually make it work. In fact, most people will like the new system better than the old one, so they won't use the safety net. Ironically, by initially providing a safety net, we create conditions that make it unlikely the safety net will actually be needed and used. However, if we don't provide the safety net, then people will resist the change; they'll fail in the new setting, and then we'll have to create a safety net to deal with the mess—and we'll have to use it. So, if we have it, we won't need it, and if we don't have it, we'll need it. It's just like an umbrella."

Charles and Susan grinned at the simile, and Doug wrote on the chart:

– By providing a safety net

"The other way to reduce resistance to change is to lessen compulsion," Doug explained. "So whenever we can, we start the transition to GEM with pilot projects and teams of volunteers. The people who volunteer will be excited about the new ideas and want to make them work. With training and a safety net, they're likely to be successful. Consequently, others will want to get involved too, because everyone loves to be part of a success. Resistance to the change evaporates."

Doug looked at his companions triumphantly. "It's all very easy when we do it right," he insisted. "People don't resist change, they resist risk and compulsion—and they're right to do so. The resistance isn't to what's being done, it's to how it's being done. If we simply change how we approach managing the change, then everything is likely to go much more smoothly."

Doug wrote on the flip chart:

- *Use volunteers as often as possible*

"That's very helpful, Doug," Susan said with grudging admiration. "But the transition to GEM is a revolutionary change."

She paused and waited for Doug's reaction.

"Yes, it is," he agreed.

"Then doesn't it have to be done by revolutionary means?" Susan asked. "Don't you have to do it quickly, forcefully, comprehensively, so that opponents don't get a chance to organize to thwart your plans?"

"No, I don't think that's necessary," Doug answered. "You can achieve revolutionary change by evolutionary means—in fact, it's often the best way. Trying to be revolutionary about it maximizes both the risk people see in the change and the compulsion they confront, and both maximize resistance."

"I hope you're right," Susan responded, "because I'm going to do what you suggest."

On the flip chart Doug had written:

When Change Is Accompanied By

Risk

and

Compulsion

People Resist It.

How to Reduce Resistance to Change
- *Eliminate the perception of risk*
  - *—By training people well*
  - *—By providing a safety net*
- *Use volunteers as often as possible*

Chapter 13

Applying GEM to Your Business

Charles and Susan had scheduled one final meeting in their series about GEM management. But in the week prior to that meeting, Susan held a two-day session for the managers of the retail business for which she had now assumed full responsibility. She gathered them in the conference room and began by preparing them for the session's first day, during which they would hear from Doug Royal and other instructors.

She had prepared an outline of some remarks and now elaborated on it. Briefly she described GEM management, then introduced Doug, who would later describe the concept in great detail.

"This is a modern technology—a technology of management," Susan began. "It's a soft technology, but a technology nonetheless. Every manager must know how to apply it. It's a new alternative which belongs in every manager's tool kit. There are six techniques to be mastered: fault tolerance, trust building, vision, goal-setting, measurement, and motivation.

"Some of these techniques are applicable beyond this single management style, GEM. They can be of great use even in the traditional directive approaches to management. But each of the six is crucial in GEM.

"Why has the new style been developed?" she asked rhetorically. "There are three reasons: economic, human, and technological."

She wrote on the flip chart that she and Charles had used so often:

Drivers or Causes of GEM

- *Economic Forces*
- *Human Aspirations*
- *Technological Progress*

"I want to give you a few examples," Susan told her listeners. "I've taken some instances from a few industries other than our own. I think this is important because I want you to know that we're not alone. Other people in other companies are trying to do exactly what we're going to be trying to do. It's unfamiliar to us all, so it's helpful for each of us to know that we have company on this journey.

"The American apparel industry has been declining very quickly under the pressure of foreign competition. It has been said for years in the industry that it has a half-life in the United States of one year; that is, every year half the remaining firms go out business, and half the jobs are lost. As a result, today it's a mere shadow of its former self, although some of the industry still struggles to survive.

"The companies and the unions involved have tried many different methods to save themselves. They've invested with MIT in an effort to develop new technology that will give them an advantage over foreign competitors. They've also turned to the new management style.

"At a shirt-making factory in Georgia, one company and the union left a highly autocratic traditional system and went to empowered teams. Supervisors were pulled away. Workers were reorganized in teams and given control of scheduling, assignments, and quality. Because the plant had been a highly monitored and very efficient one in the old style, there was ample data by which to measure the impact of the change. The organizational switch alone—there was no significant new technology—improved productivity forty percent.

"It appears that even without new technology the new management style can make manufacturing more competitive with firms abroad. For example, a tire company built a new plant in

132

the Southwest using the best available technology. Empowered teams were created, and the management relied on the GEM style, although they didn't have a label for it and didn't understand it as fully as we do now. The plant quickly became the most efficient in the world and produced the highest-quality tires on the market. So we know that combined with new hard technology, the new style in management is creating outstanding manufacturing plants. But successful applications haven't been limited to manufacturing.

"The research and development lab at a major computer company needed to reduce drastically the time it was taking to get new products into manufacturing. Already at the peak of efficiency in the traditional style, the people involved shifted to self-managing teams, labeling their effort: 'eliminating hierarchy.' And it worked. By this example, we learn that even without new hard technology, the new management style can improve performance in technical and professional units drastically.

"So GEM management, when conducted properly (unfortunately it is often done haphazardly—as we shall see later), has been ringing up a substantial record of successes. Why has this happened?

"One key reason is that empowerment is the surface reflection of a bigger and deeper movement among people in our society: a movement for greater self-realization.

"The key to the explosive strength of empowerment for improving a person's satisfaction and performance lies in fitting the person's work and personal life into a larger context. At the deeper level, empowerment reflects a different way of relating to others and to oneself—a way of being positive about life, of rejecting the disillusionment that inevitably occurs and that so often become a reason for bitterness and retreat. Since the contest between a positive attitude and a negative one occurs in both a person's personal life and business life, empowerment occurs in both areas of a person's life too. It finds opportunity in the world around us and strives to seize it. In business, freedom is limited by a person's supervisor; in private life, by the scars a person bears from having experienced life's hardships. When a person is freed of these limitations, he or she is empowered.

"The gains for a company that adopts GEM come largely from a vastly more efficient use of resources and much faster reaction to changing customer wants. When a company goes to GEM, it can reduce its staff dramatically, or can handle much more work with its existing staff. In an empowered organization it is no longer necessary to have a large bureaucracy supervising those who carry out work for customers.

"Much of a firm's workforce is a bureaucracy that performs unnecessary work. It isn't that people aren't busy; they are. Administrators keep each other and employees active answering their seemingly limitless appetite for reports and forms, but it isn't productive work. As Jack Welch, the chairman of General Electric, has said, 'Productivity advances in the future will come largely from freeing employees to quit doing unnecessary work.'"

Susan paused.

"I've given you examples from several different industries, but none from our own. Many of you must be asking yourself, 'Does this suit us, or not?'

"The question is a good one, but it is premature to attempt an answer. Too much has yet to be learned about the strengths and limitations of GEM. In virtually every industry, some department in some company is experimenting with it today. In every function—sales, order processing, insurance claims, assembly lines, personnel, finance, information services, and logistical support—GEM is being explored somewhere. When we know where it can be made to work and where it can't, then we'll be able to answer the question of where it fits and where it doesn't.

"Meanwhile, we need to make the effort to put GEM to work for us. We have a great deal to gain and probably not much to lose except the time and effort. To make the transformation successful, we must establish in our division five elements: empowered teams, new goals, new measurements, new technology, and new employee attitudes and behavior. It won't be easy, and it'll take time to make the transformation, but we can do it—and we'll have to do it if we're to be successful."

Susan paused to let her audience know she had finished; then she introduced Doug.

"I also have some preliminary comments to make," he began. "They will supplement what Susan has already said." He defined the three modern management styles for them, taking care to clearly distinguish GEM from its two ODS predecessors. He provided an outline on a second flip chart as he described the alternative management styles, moving to the chart with Susan's notations on it when he was finished. Once there, he added below what Susan had written:

The Power of GEM in the New Business Environment

- ### Cost reduction

"In an empowered organization," Doug said, "it's unnecessary to have a bureaucracy supervising those who work; instead, an environment is created for people or teams to supervise themselves. Supervisors who have been paid to watch others work can be released to work in a more productive manner, and the costs of doing business drop. In addition, empowered teams are very likely to develop more efficient and productive methods of work. So cost savings come from reductions in overhead and bureaucracy, and from better ways of working." He wrote:

- ### Psychological satisfaction

"The GEM management style also has positive psychological effects on employees compared to its ODS counterpart," Doug continued. "It gives people more freedom; it treats them like adults; it provides a greater opportunity for achievement and reward."

- ### Responsiveness to customers

"Customers are demanding more of us," Doug said. "Traditional management, with its specialization, tends to make customers the responsibility of salespeople and customer satisfaction staff. Ensuring a high degree of customer awareness requires

135

creating cross-functional teams of employees with responsibilities for meeting customer needs.

"Employees working with customers must have authority to make decisions previously reserved for management and to tap diverse sources of information to do so. Any of us questioning such a conclusion should ask ourselves the following questions: Why shouldn't employees responsible for the same customer be free to interact directly? Why should communication move through functional management on its way between members of a customer team? Don't these extra steps impede responsiveness?" Doug ended emphatically: "Of course they do."

• *Faster decision-making*

"ODS imposes tight restrictions on information sharing, confining it to the vertical channels that mark a hierarchical organization. This does not happen by accident; it is in these channels that data are reconciled and coordinated in an orderly but slow process. The critical assumption underlying this approach is that executives tend to make better decisions than those lower in the organization. Even if this is true, the process is slow and expensive.

"Historically, the deliberate pace of ODS decision-making was not a serious handicap to business. The business environment was relatively stable. Today's environment, however, is far more uncertain. Speed of decision making is at a premium. GEM, by delegating decision making to lower points in the organization and by preparing people for the challenge of making decisions, provides the power of faster decision-making."

Doug wrote:

• *New technology*

"Susan has told me that the division will be investing in a PC-based local area network. It will allow us to alter our communication patterns by linking people without regard for hierarchical position. In fact, our LAN will permit the transfer of data without engaging the hierarchy at all. This promises to improve our decision making since we'll be able to move information internally with far greater ease than in the past.

"You may be asking yourself, Why does having a LAN mean that we need a new management style? It's a good question, and it has a persuasive answer. LAN communication channels, with their ability to skip levels or cross functions, may end up excluding key managers from the flow of data. Firms using the ODS management style cannot allow the loss of control of information in this fashion because *their managers continue to make all decisions.* Leaving decision-making power in the hands of people who might lack the data to do so—even when those people are managers—invites chaos.

"See how much impact the LAN is likely to have on our way of working?" Doug asked. "It will spread information and communication so that rank-and-file people can have up-to-the-minute information upon which to base decisions, and it will deny aggregated, previously analyzed data to management for its decision making. This is because digesting the data will consume time and resources that a least-cost organization will lack. So the LAN will tend to stand our organization on its head. To make effective use of the new technology, we have to adopt the new management style."

With a flourish of his arms, Doug gave final emphasis to his point: "As this technological revolution unfolds, it will require that we use GEM."

After a pause to let his statement sink in, Doug said, "I have one final point to make today. I've been talking about what GEM is and what we can gain from it, but now I want to do something that's unusual for a trainer. I want to tell you how to make GEM fail—or at least how to ensure that the transformation of our division to GEM will fail."

Doug wrote on the chart:

How to Make GEM Fail

"The first wrong step," Doug began, "is to have no goals or to set the wrong goals. This will kill the new management style quickly. Empowered teams will act. If they have no goals or the wrong goals, they'll quickly mess up the business. It's a great mistake for a firm to empower people who don't have clear, appropriate goals. Unfortunately, it's done often."

He wrote on the chart:

- *Set the wrong goals.*

"The second wrong step," Doug continued, "is to have the wrong measures. This will kill GEM slowly as people come to realize that management cannot distinguish success from failure and, therefore, rewards the wrong teams. The system will slowly strangle on demoralization."

He wrote:

- *Use the wrong measures.*

"The third wrong step is to skimp on training in order to save money. This will cause GEM to collapse almost instantaneously."

"Why?" a listener spoke up.

"Because most people don't know how to work in an empowered environment," Doug answered. "They're used to waiting for instructions from supervisors as to how to proceed. Without training that clarifies what is expected of them, they'll wait for directions, and with no supervisors to give directions, everything will just stand still."

"But no company would do that," objected Doug's questioner.

"Of course it would," Doug responded with a grin. "Companies do it all the time. There's a reason for it. The company is probably in competitive difficulty, which is why it's going to GEM in the first place. It's trying to cut its costs, improve its quality, and enhance its responsiveness to customers. So it decides it can save money—which it desperately needs—by skimping on training. As a consequence of insufficient training, the whole effort collapses before it's really underway, and the company's much worse off than if it had never considered GEM in the first place.

"In fact, trying GEM but leaving out a crucial element is so common that it explains most of the failures that have occurred. Often I meet business executives who say they tried empowerment and it failed. If I ask them to tell me about the experience in detail, most of the time it turns out that they tried to save money by cutting corners on training, so that people didn't know what they were supposed to do in an empowered team—and did nothing. The result? Failure!"

On the chart Doug wrote:

- *Don't train the people.*

"Next . . ." Doug began, but Susan, watching from the back of the room, saw that her team was wearing out. Motioning to Doug, she walked to the front of the room.

"What this means," Susan explained to her team, "is that the only reason for ultimate failure is unclear goals or failure to meet the other basic conditions. We won't be able to blame the incompetence or lack of motivation on our people. The responsibility for making an empowered environment work rests with us, and we've no excuses for failure. With Doug's help, we've learned how to make it work as well as how to make it fail. Which course of action we follow is our choice—and our responsibility."

She thanked Doug and then told her audience: "Tomorrow we'll split into small groups. We've done a lot today, and now I want us to debrief it. I've learned," and she directed a grateful glance toward Doug, "that for people to really internalize or own a set of concepts they must be given time to question them, restate them, and thereby fix them in their minds. So I have this assignment for your teams for tonight and tomorrow morning: first, identify the most important concepts we've learned; second, decide which of the concepts can be put to effective use in our business; third, create a plan of action for where we should start in applying these ideas when we return to our own offices the day after tomorrow."

Susan displayed the assignment on a screen, and when everyone had copied it, she dismissed the meeting. As the crowd streamed from the room, she studied the notes she and Doug had made during the course of the day's presentations. She went to the chart and added to some of the categories. Doug watched her and periodically nodded his approval.

Drivers or Causes of GEM

- *Economic Forces*
  - *Rapid change*
  - *Intense competition*
- *Human Aspirations*
  - *For more independence*
  - *For greater rewards for performance*
- *Technological Progress*
  - *Computer networks*
  - *Distribution computing*
  - *Data-base accessibility*

The Power of GEM in the New Business Environment

- *Cost reduction*
- *Psychological satisfaction*
- *Responsiveness to customers*
- *Faster decision-making*
- *New technology*

How to Make GEM Fail

- *Set the wrong goals.*
- *Use the wrong measures.*
- *Don't train the people.*

Chapter 14

Making a Personal Commitment

Susan was packing when Charles wandered into her office.

"When are you going?" he asked her.

"Tomorrow."

"We'll miss you here," Charles told her warmly.

"You're very nice to say so," Susan responded with a smile.

"Do you want to be at the division headquarters?" Charles asked. "You know, you could stay here."

"I guess I could," Susan admitted, "but I feel I ought to be with the division. You know, we don't have many managers now that we're going to GEM, so I should be there to support my people."

"That's what a leader would do," Charles grinned.

"Yeah," Susan replied ruefully. "There are so few of us in executive positions that we have to be leaders—we haven't the time to be managers."

Charles laughed. "I thought all the talk about our being leaders and not administrators was really only talk," he said, "until GEM came along and gave executives so much responsibility and so large a group of subordinates that we had to stop managing and start leading."

"Yes," Susan said. "What's that old saying? 'There's nothing like the prospect of a hanging to concentrate the mind.'"

"Susan!" Charles burst out in mock surprise. "What a thing to say!"

"Well, it's true, isn't it?" she replied. "I have this division to run. My goals are bigger than my predecessor's, but my resources have been downsized. So I'm either going to find a smarter way to run the place, or I'm going to collapse while trying to do it the

141

old way. The hanging's going to be mine—at least my career's—if I can't concentrate enough to make the new system work. I'm convinced that in today's business climate, it's GEM or nothing."

Charles laughed. "That's where we started our discussions months ago, isn't it? Except then I had the problem of deciding whether I should go see Ron Jackson or Philip Kowalski, remember? That turned out well for me. Cardenas was delighted with my exercise of initiative. Now you have the problem of deciding how to run your division."

"I guess turnabout is fair play," she answered, returning to her packing.

"You know," Charles ventured, "I've very much enjoyed these discussions with you. I think I gained a lot from them."

She again turned to face him. "I did, too." Noticing that he seemed unwilling to leave, she also made a suggestion. "Maybe we should keep in touch. We're both experimenting with GEM, and it's unfamiliar to most of our superiors and peers in the company. We could use each other's support."

Charles grinned; he seemed to have been waiting for this. "Yes, I agree," he said quickly. "I suggest a bond between us—a commitment to press ahead. We'll bring in others if they become interested. And Doug is already with us, of course."

"Yes, of course," Susan agreed.

"After all," Charles continued, "in a sense, we are the company. I mean, the firm has all its plants, products, and brand names, as well as its financial and physical assets, but if you really think about it, in an environment as competitive as today's, those things erode very quickly. A top-notch competitor could throw our business in the tank very quickly—unless . . ."

Charles paused suspensefully. Susan listened intently for him to continue, but as the pause lengthened, she asked, "Unless . . . unless what?"

"Unless we who work in the company use all those assets in a smart and effective way," Charles concluded his statement. "No company can just sit on its assets today, because there are too many competitors anxious to take the business away from them. All our facilities and financial assets are like tools handed down to us from the past, for us to use well or badly. If we use them badly, then nothing will protect this company from failure. If we use them well, then our company will grow and prosper. And it's up to us to do it, for if we don't do it, who else will?"

"That's very eloquent, Charles," Susan complimented him.

An embarrassed smile flickered around his mouth. "What sort of bond should we have between us?" he asked her.

"First," Susan suggested, "let's agree to master GEM."

Charles went to the board and wrote:

Our Intent

To Learn . . .

- *The different management styles*
- *GEM*

He stopped and looked to Susan for a suggestion. She picked up a marker and added to the list:

- *Fault tolerance*
- *Three levels of trust*
- *How to manage change*

"Very good!" Charles exclaimed. Standing beside her at the board, he wrote:

Our "To Do's"

- *Use ODS and GEM models to clarify our thinking*
- *Build empowered teams*
- *Lead, not administer*

Now Susan added:

- *Guide others as we transform the organization*

And Charles wrote:

- *Guide others as we transform ourselves*

They admired their work.

"We need a personal commitment plan," Charles announced suddenly.

"Really?" Susan asked, her eyes widening.

Determined to push ahead, Charles wrote:

Personal Commitment Plan

- *Challenge the conventional.*
- *Think through issues, not just about them.*
- *Try to reduce bureaucracy.*

"I see what you have in mind," Susan said, her voice rising in excitement. "I agree that we need one. And we ought to see if other people will sign on to it."

Charles nodded in agreement as she added to his list:

- *Think beyond traditional boundaries.*

Charles reached in to add:

- *Involve others.*

And Susan wrote:

- *Truly empower.*

"Is that enough?" she asked.

"Can we sum it all up in a pithy slogan?" Charles asked.

Susan laughed. "Should we do that?"

"If we can, of course." Charles paused. "Let's see . . ." He wrote on the board:

Our Slogan
Decentralize

He paused again, then wrote:

Empower

As he hesitated yet again, Susan finished the thought:

and

Respond

"There," she said triumphantly. "How's that?"

"Great!" he replied. "There's a lot of very powerful stuff in there."

"Yes, there is. We've done a good job."

"Well, Susan," Charles said, "I'd better get along and let you finish your packing. I'm very pleased that you have this opportunity. Maybe you'll end up our CEO—then for the first time we'd have a commitment to GEM, and one based on a full understanding of it."

With that, Charles shook her hand, turned around, and left her office. Susan watched him depart with a thoughtful smile on her face. They had written on the board behind her:

Our Intent

To Learn . . .
- *The different management styles*
- *GEM*
- *Fault tolerance*
- *Three levels of trust*
- *How to manage change*

Our "To Do's"

- Use ODS and GEM models to clarify our thinking
- Build empowered teams
- Lead, not administer
- Guide others as we transform the organization
- Guide others as we transform ourselves

Our Personal Commitment Plan

- Challenge the conventional.
- Think through issues, not just about them.
- Try to reduce bureaucracy.
- Think beyond traditional boundaries.
- Involve others.
- Truly empower.

Our Slogan

Decentralize

Empower

and

Respond

About the Author

Daniel Quinn Mills, Professor of Business Administration at Harvard University, is a skilled practitioner of the art of management. He has consulted for leading corporations, including G.E., IBM, Alcoa, Sears, G.M., and Polaroid, and was a presidential appointee to The National Commission on Employment Policy. Born in 1941, Mills earned his MA and Ph.D. from Harvard, both in economics, and received his undergraduate degree from Ohio Wesleyan, which has since awarded him its Distinguished Achievement Citation. Before arriving at the Harvard Business School in 1976, he taught at MIT's Sloan Management School, receiving the Baker Award in 1971 for outstanding teaching. In 1978 his ability in the classroom was again recognized when Harvard honored him with the Albert J. Weatherhead, Jr. Professorship of Business Administration. A prolific and highly regarded writer, Mills has published numerous books, including *Rebirth of the Corporation, The IBM Lesson, Not Like Our Parents, The New Competitors, Industrial Relations in Transition,* and *Labor-Management Relations.* He is widely and often quoted in the national media, and appeared as a guest on NBC's *Today Show.*